Inside the JavaOS™ Operating System

Inside the JavaOS™ Operating System

Tom Saulpaugh
Charles Mirho

ADDISON-WESLEY

An imprint of Addison Wesley Longman, Inc.

Reading, Massachusetts • Harlow, England • Menlo Park, California
Berkeley, California • Don Mills, Ontario • Sydney
Bonn • Amsterdam • Tokyo • Mexico City

Many of the designations used by the manufacturers and sellers to distinguish their products are claimed as trademarks. When those designations appear in this book and Addison-Wesley was aware of a trademark claim, the designations have been printed in initial caps or all caps.

The authors and publisher have taken care in the preparation of this book, but make no expressed or implied warranty of any kind and assume no responsibility for errors or omissions. No liability is assumed for incidental or consequential damages in connection with or arising out of the use of the information or programs contained herein.

The publisher offers discounts on this book when ordered in quantity for special sales. For more information, please contact:

Corporate, Government, and Special Sales Group
Addison Wesley Longman, Inc.
One Jacob Way
Reading, Massachusetts 01867

Library of Congress Cataloging-in-publication Data
Saulpaugh, Tom
    Inside the JavaOS™ Operating System, Tom Saulpaugh,
    Charles Mirho.
            p.   cm.
    Includes index.
    ISBN 0-201-18393-5
    1. JavaOS™ operating system.   2. Operating systems (Computers)   3. Java
(Computer programming language)   I. Mirho, Charles A.   II. Title.
QA76.76.063S3563   1999
005.4'469--dc21   98-51423
                                                                  CIP

ISBN 0-201-18393-5
Text printed on recycled and acid-free paper.

1 2 3 4 5 6 7 8 9 10 – MA – 03 02 01 00 99
First Printing, January 1999

Contents

Preface

I've been hooked on operating systems ever since I took my first OS course at Cal Poly, San Luis Obispo. I was lucky enough to land a job right after graduating, in 1982, working on operating systems for Digital Research Inc. (DRI) in Monterey, California.

In June of 1985, I joined Apple's MacOS group. Apple enjoyed tremendous growth from 1985 to 1990. Each new release of the OS added more functionality (QuickDraw in color, 32-bit addressing, SCSI bus support) for more and more flavors of Macintosh. The pace of addition was staggering, so much so that Apple never had time to recode the low-level OS and fix some of its shortcomings.

By 1990, these shortcomings, including no preemptive multitasking and no memory protection for applications, began to affect the quality of the product. The Mac was the easiest computer to use but also one of the most fragile. Mac users quickly learned the location of the reboot button on the back of the box.

In June of 1990, I had lunch with Bill Bruffey of the MacOS group. Bill is a great engineer who designed the Mac's innovative file system—the Hierarchical File System (HFS). Bill had grown tired of waiting for Taligent to produce a new MacOS and he had received permission to build a new microkernel, called NuKernel, tuned for the Macintosh operating system.

He envisioned a microkernel that ran Mac applications in a virtual machine and supported a new modern concurrent input/output (I/O) system. Bill hired me as employee number one on a project that was eventually known as Copland.

Fred Brooks could easily write a modern version of *The Mythical Man-Month* about the Copland project. Copland started lean and mean, with Bill hiring just four more engineers during that first year. After just a few months of work, we five demonstrated to management a microkernel-based MacOS running on a MacII-ci. The project gained steam over the next few years and eventually grew to more than 500 employees, and Bill and I became two contributing engineers with no management authority.

Somewhere during the middle of the Copland project, management asked me to back-port some Copland I/O technology to a new family of Macintosh computers sporting the PCI expansion bus. I took a year off from the Copland project and helped Apple ship a PowerPC-native device driver architecture for its new PCI-based Macs.

The PCI team was focused and lean. A small team of engineers built and deployed a large amount of software in a year's time with none of the bureaucratic overhead of the Copland project. My time working on PCI for System 7.5 proved to be the most enjoyable year of my Apple career.

When I returned to the Copland project in June of 1995, I found a mess. The Copland leadership had decided to recode the toolbox and break popular existing system extensions such as After Dark. Apple had gambled that users and developers wouldn't mind a new OS that wasn't a hundred percent backward compatible! I made up my mind that summer to leave Apple.

In May of 1995, Sun Microsystems introduced Java at SunWorld. As the Java phenomenon materialized over the next six months, Jim Mitchell and Peter Madany of Sun's JavaSoft began to build a new OS (code-named Kona) to run only Java software.

I was hired in March of 1996 to design an I/O architecture for Kona, soon to be renamed JavaOS™. The early Kona team consisted of seven people. The team was extremely focused and produced the first official release of the JavaOS operating system in just 15 months. After my experience with the Copland project, I felt lucky and honored to be working with bright, focused people on an innovative operating system.

In early 1997, JavaSoft handed over control of JavaOS to SunSoft. Late that year, the SunSoft JavaOS team, headed by Bob Rodriguez, began working closely with an IBM team to build the next release of JavaOS, eventually renamed JavaOS for Business™. The contributions from IBM were significant and included many key architectural features.

This book provides an inside look at the results of Sun's and IBM's efforts to build a new thin-client operating system. The book uses the name JavaOS throughout, but the version of the JavaOS operating system presented here is JavaOS for Business.

Tom Saulpaugh
Senior Staff Engineer
Sun Microsystems, Inc.

When I first learned about the JavaOS operating system, I was a second-year, part-time law student at Santa Clara University, with a full-time job writing patents during the day. The last thing I needed was another distraction in my life. But I have always been fascinated by operating systems, which I consider the most intricate and complex software programs on the planet. A new operating system based around, and written in, the Java programming language was intriguing. Think of the possibilities: system services loaded on demand and distributed execution between client and server, or even on multiple clients and multiple servers! A single OS code base, regardless of client or server hardware architecture, residing in a central location. An end to complicated software upgrades—simply *subscribe* to your operating system and applications, and the latest upgrades and bug fixes magically appear each time you boot up. These are some of the possibilities opened up by JavaOS technology.

When I first met Tom Saulpaugh, he was an Apple Computer refugee who had just recently joined JavaSoft. The JavaOS team was only about ten people, and there was a sense that the rest of JavaSoft didn't see the potential of this new technology. Someone needed to get the word out. Tom, myself, and a hard-driving Sun technical writer, Tom Clements, set out to do just that. First came an article in *BYTE* magazine, a bit of undisguised evangelism. Next a meeting with James Gosling, at which we pitched the merits of JavaOS with regards to the Java language itself. Things started to happen.

A Sun product group took responsibility for the JavaOS operating system from JavaSoft, Chorus was purchased for their microkernel technology, IBM signed on to co-develop and market JavaOS, and the team grew. I'm certainly not going to take credit for making JavaOS a success; I was mostly an outsider looking in, but I like to think my early enthusiasm had some impact on getting folks to stand up and take notice. It is safe to say that the time for a book on JavaOS has arrived.

Inside the JavaOS™ *Operating System* is about using Java technology to make an operating system simpler, more reliable, more powerful, and easier to maintain. In this spirit of simplicity and power, we have tried to create a book that explains the workings of JavaOS in simple, concise terms. This was not always easy, because operating systems are by their nature obscure and complex beasts. I hope you enjoy reading about JavaOS as much as we enjoyed writing about it.

Charles Mirho

Acknowledgments

This book was two years in the making. It was written as the software was developed and has changed many times. Along the way, the following people have contributed to its content: Jeff Schmidt, Anne Bluntschli, Tom Clements, Bill Kain, and Bruce Montague.

Among the tremendous engineering talent from Sun who worked on this operating system are: Rajeev Bharadhwaj, Bob Rodriguez, Ron Karim, Dennis Aaron, Mohamed Abdelaziz, Angela Byrum, Jagane Sundar, Rich Berlin, Nedim Fresko, Mike Shoemaker, Dean Long, Graham Hamilton, Lisa Stark-Berryman, Greg Slaughter, Bill Keenan, Jason Li, Tom Mason, Tim Sia, Don Hudson, Ed Goei, Bernard Traversat, Sam Yan, Eric Yeh, and Mercia Zheng.

A special thanks goes to two Sun individuals, Bob Delaney and Ron Kleinman, who provided valuable insight into the operating system's feature set.

Steve Woodward, Bill Tracey, Mike Sullivan, Jonathan Wagner, Sheila Harnett, Joe Tano, and Les Wilson were among the great IBM engineering contributors.

Above all, thanks to Maureen, Matthew, Evan, Rachel, and Erika and Max for their encouragement and support.

Introduction

Why a New OS?

JavaOS™ is a new commercial operating system (OS) developed by Sun Microsystems, Inc., and IBM. A commercial operating system is perhaps the most complicated piece of software anyone can endeavor to build and maintain.

Once deployed, a successful operating system takes on a life of its own. Device drivers, tools, and applications are built to take advantage of the new OS. In turn, the OS is bug-fixed and expanded to reward early software developers with more functionality and, if all goes well, more performance and reliability. Early pioneering users are asked to be patient as the system matures. Typically any operating system does not mature until its third major release.

Today, companies such as IBM, Microsoft, Apple, and Sun Microsystems put so much time, effort, and money into developing, enhancing, and maintaining an OS that very few new operating systems are built any more. Simply put, in the current market there must be a compelling reason to build a new commercial OS.

Yesterday's Reason: A New Hardware Architecture

In the past, new commercial operating systems typically were created to take advantage of the power of a new computer hardware architecture, or platform. As you know, a computer's architecture, consisting of the set of attributes that determine what software will run on the computer, is used as a blueprint to *build* the computer.

New computer architectures were created when significantly greater functionality and performance become possible with a new family of "iron." By far, the most common reason to build a new computer-hardware architecture was to deliver more memory-addressing capability, such as Digital Equipment Corporation's introduction of the VAX architecture.

Computer-addressing capability is measured by the size, in bits, of an address. A 32-bit address, for example, yields 4GB of addressable memory space, or *address space*. A 32-bit address space enables a computer to run larger and more complex applications than is possible with, say, a 16-bit address space.

Today's Reason: Java™ Technology

In the 1970s, IBM and Digital Equipment Corporation helped to standardize the business and scientific computing worlds. In the 1980s, Apple, IBM, and Microsoft introduced standardized personal computing to the individual, and Sun introduced the workstation.

The decade of the 1980s saw a tremendous consolidation of computing based on this evolving set of common standards. These standards, because of their value to the consumer, permeated to the deepest levels of the platform—the CPU and devices.

The IBM PC architecture was defined in 1981; the turbo-charged PC of today is a superset of that original architecture. The burden of supporting years of legacy hardware and software products grows with each year that passes. Surprisingly, while hardware has advanced by leaps and bounds, operating system technology has progressed more slowly. Most operating systems today are still written largely in C, C++, and assembly code. These software technologies place a practical limit on what the OS can do.

The Java programming language opens new possibilities in OS design. A large portion of the system software is entirely insulated from the underlying platform. This enables a degree of standardization, centralization, and footprint customization that was simply impractical with native code OSs. It also enables a more secure and robust OS environment because of the Java programming language's inherent fail-safe features.

JavaOS for Business™ represents the most advanced JavaOS implementation, and many of the technologies described in this book were implemented first there. Already, some JavaOS technologies have found there way into other environments. The JavaOS System Database and the portions of the device driver architecture are good examples of this, having found there way into point-of-sale applications.

How This Book Is Organized

This book takes a high-level look at the JavaOS operating system but does not cover specific programming interfaces in great detail. The JavaOS design is presented top-down, beginning at the highest level and progressing layer by layer more deeply into the operating system. The reader is assumed to be familiar with the Java programming language and with the Java Development Kit (JDK).

Chapter 1, Introduction, explores the evolution of JavaOS from a simple stand-alone Java Virtual Machine (JVM) to a modern, microkernel-based operating system.

Chapter 2, The Database, covers the JavaOS System Database (JSD) which may be used to configure the operating system.

Chapter 3, Events, presents the JavaOS Event System which may be used to support automatic plug-and-play devices.

Chapter 4, Service Loader, presents the JavaOS Service Loader (JSL) which may be used to load operating system services such as device drivers.

Chapter 5, Standard Device Support, gives information on support for standard JDK devices, such as network and graphic devices.

Chapter 6, Device Drivers, gives an overview of the JavaOS Device Interface (JDI) and JavaOS device driver architecture.

Chapter 7, Memory, presents the JavaOS memory model.

Chapter 8, Interrupts, covers the JavaOS interrupt model.

Chapter 9, The Microkernel, covers the JavaOS microkernel.

Chapter 10, Booting, presents the JavaOS boot architecture and the JavaOS Boot Interface (JBI).

Chapter 1
Overview

The JavaOS™ software is a new operating system (OS) optimized to run software written in the Java™ programming language on a variety of devices, from embedded platforms to network computers. (We use the term "JavaOS" in place of "JavaOS operating system" throughout this text.) As an alternative to hosting the Java Development Kit (JDK) on a native OS, JavaOS provides a standalone JDK hosting environment. More than two-thirds of JavaOS is written in the Java programming language, with the remainder written in C and a small assembly language component.

Because JavaOS is new, it provides a minimal implementation for hosting the JDK. There is no extra code in the system for supporting legacy applications. Because a large portion of the OS is software written in the Java programming language (which we shall refer to as simply "Java software"), JavaOS is object-oriented and portable. As you will learn later in this chapter, JavaOS may serve as an "incubator," gradually reducing the amount of native code necessary for hosting the JDK.

1.1 Evolution of JavaOS

JavaOS began its existence as a platform for embedded devices. James Gosling, working for Sun Microsystems, created a small runtime environment and language definition for enabling cross-platform programming on small, consumer electronic devices. Gosling designed Java as an interpreted language running on a virtual machine, a software central processing unit (CPU) with its own instruction set. In essence, this virtual machine created an abstraction of the physical CPU that programs could target in a device-independent way.

In addition to the Java Virtual Machine (JVM), the Java Runtime Environment included a garbage collector (GC) for reclaiming system resources and a class loader for loading and preparing objects for execution. It also included "core" classes for supporting the Java programming language definition and for the convenience of application programs.

From these rudimentary building blocks, all subsequent versions of the JDK and JavaOS have evolved. Figure 1.1 illustrates a generalized view of the early Java platform.

The Java Runtime Environment, the middle software layer in Figure 1.1, is the collection of software components (Java Virtual Machine, garbage collector, class loader, classes, and so on) that form the Java software execution environment.

The classes are divided into OS-independent and OS-dependent kinds. Core classes have no dependency on the underlying operating system (they contain no native method declarations), while host classes contain native method declarations, forcing the underlying OS to implement some service (thread support, for example).

JavaOS and the JDK have evolved in parallel. The JDK evolved to enhance the performance of the Java Runtime Environment and the set of available APIs developers use to write platform-independent Java software.

JavaOS has evolved the host classes to enhance the portability of the runtime layer by increasing the amount of Java software found in that layer. The increased amount of Java software in the runtime environment eliminates the need for a big, native host operating system because the runtime layer includes services such as device drivers and platform configuration.

As the JDK evolves and expands its functionality, JavaOS expands to meet the JDK's new hosting requirements. Figure 1.2 illustrates the separate, but parallel, evolution of JavaOS and the JDK.

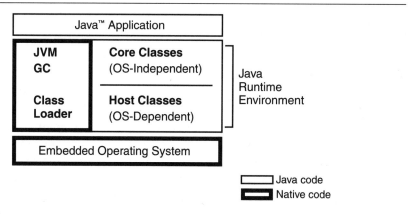

FIGURE 1.1 *The Early Java Platform*

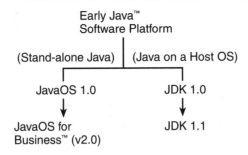

FIGURE 1.2 *JDK and JavaOS Evolution*

To host the JDK, JavaOS provides an implementation of the hosting classes (low- and middle-level windowing and graphics code, network protocol stacks, and so on) normally provided by a host OS such as Solaris.

In addition to supporting the standard JDK hosting classes, JavaOS includes system services specifically tuned to the needs of the host classes and Java software. (A host operating system also runs non-Java programs; thus, the services are not tuned with Java software needs in mind.)

JavaOS provides system services, such as device drivers, as well as basic infra-structure, such as interrupt management and an event notification mechanism. Some of the system services discussed in this book are:

- A system configuration database
- An event system
- A demand-based service loader
- A device manager (for managing device drivers)

JavaOS provides an expanded runtime environment that does not require a large native host OS to execute Java applications. Only a simple microkernel is required to host the JavaOS Runtime Environment, not an entire OS. Figure 1.3 illustrates Java hosted by a host OS. Notice in particular the runtime environment, consisting of the JVM, GC, class loader, classes, developer APIs, and the native hosting code for graphics, I/O, networking, and system services.

As Figure 1.3 makes clear, the JDK hosted on a typical native OS is a largely horizontal API layer that depends on the host OS for much of its implementation.

By comparison, Figure 1.4 illustrates the JDK hosted on JavaOS. Compare this figure to the preceding one, noticing in particular the expanded runtime environment. It is apparent that much of the hosting code is now written in the Java programming language, creating a full-blown Java technology operating system, not merely a horizontal Java API layer.

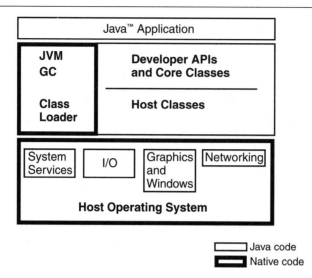

FIGURE 1.3   *JDK Hosted on a Host OS*

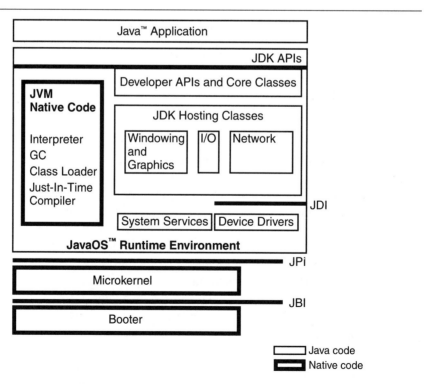

FIGURE 1.4   *JavaOS—Standalone JDK Hosting*

The JavaOS Runtime Environment is only one component (although the largest one) of JavaOS itself. Although the JavaOS Runtime Environment does not require a host OS, it does require a microkernel for the more basic OS functionality, including support for threads, interrupts, monitors, and low-level memory management. JavaOS also includes a booter to get up and running. The microkernel and booter are discussed in detail in Chapters 9 and 10.

One of the more important features in JavaOS is the JavaOS Platform Interface (JPI). The JPI is a collection of classes and interfaces that abstract the services of the microkernel from the rest of the JavaOS Runtime Environment so that the runtime can be ported to a variety of microkernels. This unique feature of JavaOS enables it to function with best-of-breed microkernels on everything from embedded platforms to network computers. The JPI is further explained in Chapters 6, 7, and 8.

1.2   JavaOS and the JDK

The roadmap for JavaOS closely parallels and interacts with the roadmap of the JDK. The JDK continues to expand, incorporating more APIs for the convenience of Java application programmers. Meanwhile, JavaOS expands to meet the new hosting requirements of the JDK. In the future, the cross-platform hosting classes in JavaOS might find their way into subsequent versions of the JDK, enabling the JDK to be hosted at a lower level on a host OS and increasing the amount of Java software in these systems.

Of course, it is up to the JDK group in Sun Microsystems to decide which classes actually become part of the JDK. Figure 1.5 illustrates this cyclical relationship.

The Java Platform Services (JPS) exemplifies how JavaOS serves as an incubator for useful Java technology. The JPS is a collection of JavaOS services that, when used in a standard JDK environment, enable vertical applications for point of sale (POS), ATMs, and travel kiosks, to name just a few.

The JPS includes three JavaOS services: the database, the service loader, and the event system. JPS also provides device access by way of the Java Comm API.

FIGURE 1.5   *Technology Cycle of the JDK and JavaOS*

Each of the JavaOS services included in the JPS code package (a .JAR file) is written in the Java programming language. Thus, the JPS JAR file may be used in any JDK environment, whether hosted on Windows™, DOS™, Solaris™, Mac™, JavaPC™ software, or any embedded OS. For example, the JPS can be added to an old x86 processor-based computer running JavaPC™ software to create an inexpensive network-managed travel kiosk.

1.3 Supported Computing Models

JavaOS is designed to work in a variety of computing models. Each of these computing models has certain benefits and drawbacks, particularly in terms of manageability, speed of execution, and network traffic. JavaOS supports the following computing models:

- Operating system cached on the client, executed on the client
- Operating system stored on the server, executed on the client
- Data files cached on the client
- Data files stored on the server
- Applications cached on the client, executed on the client
- Applications stored on the server, executed on the client

As you can see, JavaOS is designed for distributed processing, not server-centric processing. In other words, it is a *client* operating system. A future version of the OS might even be able to intelligently partition the execution of operating system and application code between client and server.

Although JavaOS is a client operating system, it supports both local client and network booting. The advantage of network booting is that operating system upgrades, backups, and security can be centralized at the server. The disadvantage is increased loading on the network, at least during periods when many clients are booted at once. Network booting also tends to take longer. JavaOS does support the storage of both applications and data on the server. The advantage is central maintenance; the disadvantage is increased network traffic and slower response.

Another disadvantage of accessing code and files on the network is the implicit reliance such access creates on the network connection. When the network is down, it might be impossible to access the files and applications you want to use. With these disadvantages, why would anyone want to centralize software and data files on the server? The answer is twofold. First, the expense of managing large numbers of clients, each with its own local OS and data files, outweighs the drawbacks of centralizing on the server. Second, and perhaps more importantly, a small, fast local cache can be employed in each client to eliminate or greatly reduce many of the drawbacks of centralization.

This cache can take the form of flash memory, a small, fast hard disk, or some other persistent storage device. The server downloads and caches OS classes, application classes, and data files on an as-needed basis. Download latencies and network traffic delays are incurred only once; after that, JavaOS can access the cached copy rather than going to the network. If the cache is large enough, it might be possible to disconnect from the network and go mobile without suffering downtime. Figure 1.6 illustrates the ways in which the content of the cache evolves in response to user workflow.

Early versions of JavaOS did not implement a caching facility. Caching will be implemented in a future release, along with concurrency and replacement algorithms to keep the cache filled with the latest, most necessary classes and data from the server. Notice that JavaOS employs demand-based loading of nonessential classes, so classes are not loaded from the network until they are needed. The result is that the operating system and applications can grow quite large, with integrated features and functions, without overwhelming the resources of the client.

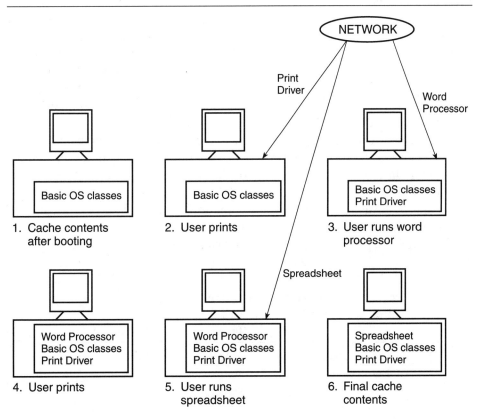

FIGURE 1.6 *Evolution of Cache Contents over Time*

At any given moment only the useful classes from the OS and applications are loaded on the client.

1.4 Code Composition

JavaOS is composed of three types of computer code:

- Native
- Hardware-independent
- Platform-independent

References to these code types appear frequently in this book. To understand how JavaOS is put together, it is necessary to understand the distinctions between the three code types.

Native code is composed of instructions in the instruction set of the native CPU. Native code is CPU-dependent and is typically a compiled or assembled form of C language or assembly language. Native code is not written in the Java programming language.

Hardware-independent code has no dependencies on specific hardware (other than perhaps the CPU) or on specific memory or I/O addresses. It does not rely on a specific bus, nor does it depend on specific device timings. Hardware-independent code can be either native code or Java software. Thus, a native method compiled from C language for computing the slope of a line will be hardware-independent, not CPU-independent.

Platform-independent code, as defined here, is code that contains no dependencies on a specific CPU, memory model, byte ordering, or interrupt implementation. Only Java software can be platform-independent; native code never can be. Platform-independent code still can depend upon specific device characteristics. For example, JavaOS device drivers written in the Java language are platform-independent but contain dependencies for a particular device and bus combination. Though independent of platform, a JavaOS device driver is still dependent on hardware. Table 1.1 summarizes these relationships.

TABLE 1.1 Three Types of JavaOS Software Code

	Java	Native
CPU-Independent	Always	Never
Hardware-Independent	Sometimes	Sometimes
Platform-Independent	Sometimes	Never

1.5 Major Components

Most major JavaOS components are part of the JavaOS Runtime Environment. Three components exist to support the runtime and, thus, are separate from it[1]:

- JPI
- Booter
- Microkernel

This book focuses on components unique to JavaOS, not on those that are currently part of the JDK, which are well documented in other publications. The remainder of this book discusses in greater detail the JavaOS Runtime Environment components mentioned here.

1.5.1 Runtime Components

The four major JavaOS Runtime Environment components are:
- The system database
- The event system
- The service loader
- Device drivers

The System Database
The JavaOS System Database (JSD) is a central repository of configuration information for the operating system, device drivers, and applications. The JSD is a structured collection of named Java objects. Naming an object is the process of associating a name (a string) with a set of values (the object's properties).

Each name and property set in the database is called an *entry*. Entries can serve to name items such as installed devices, Java programming language interfaces, users, groups of objects, or system services. Naming an object serves to advertise its existence to other software components in the system.

The JSD supports both transient and persistent information. Device information, for example, is largely transient and obtained each time a platform boots. The persistent information is *cached* locally on the platform but initially obtained

---

1. Notably absent from the JavaOS component list are the JVM, the GC, and the class loader. Although essential elements of JavaOS, these components are available as part of the standard JavaOS Runtime Environment. With the JDK, JavaOS does not require separate versions of these components. It simply uses what the JDK already supplies.

and continuously synchronized with a variety of remote backing store repositories, such as an LDAP server. Figure 1.7 illustrates the types and sources of data found in the JSD. Chapter 2 provides details on the JSD.

The Event System

The JavaOS Event System routes events from their point of origin to their point of destination within JavaOS. An event is a typed piece of information. The simplest events contain a single piece of information identifying the source of the event (the *event producer*). Events can be received by multiple clients, each of which is termed an *event consumer*.

Events are divided into categories. One category is configuration, which includes events that are generated when adding and removing entries from the JSD. Another category consists of events generated by I/O requests to drivers (buffer empty, data ready, and so on). Chapter 3 describes the event system in detail.

The Service Loader

Services are a group of Java programming language packages that advertise their capabilities in the JSD and can be located and loaded on demand. Examples of services are device drivers, network protocols, and file systems. The JavaOS Service Loader (JSL) loads and unloads services in response to demands for their advertised capabilities. The result is a client OS image that is self-optimizing to the workflow of individual users, as well as to machines.

Demand for services typically originates from Java applications. For example, an application might request printing services at a time when the print driver is not loaded. The demand is recognized by the operating system, which in turn invokes the JSL to load the required print driver from the network.Chapter 4 describes the JSL in detail.

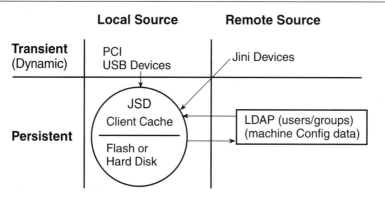

FIGURE 1.7   *JSD Data Types and Sources*

Device Drivers

Device drivers are part of the JavaOS Runtime Environment. The role of device drivers in JavaOS is to implement I/O operations. Drivers communicate with Java applications using the event system and the JavaOS Device Interface (JDI).

Drivers in JavaOS are platform-independent. Platform independence does not mean bus or hardware independence. Each device driver is written to operate with one or more buses and to service a particular device. Unlike some operating systems, JavaOS makes no attempt to abstract bus dependencies from its drivers.

Early versions of JavaOS did not contain a formal device-driver model. In later versions of JavaOS, the JPI and the JDI were created to support a formal, portable device-driver model. The JDI is a framework for supporting I/O, but it is not a heavy-handed framework. Rather, the JDI allows for unique device capabilities to be directly represented in device interfaces. Other operating systems, by contrast, often package device operations under the umbrella of a special system call, such as IOCtl.

On the other hand, an I/O system with few or no common interfaces across devices offers little value to developers. Where possible, JavaOS defines interfaces that apply to all devices or all device categories. Device events and naming also are areas where JavaOS presents unified mechanisms and policies. Chapter 6 describes device drivers in detail.

1.5.2 Non-Runtime Components

Three major components of JavaOS are essential to supporting the JavaOS Runtime Environment:

- JPI
- Booter
- Microkernel

Of the three, the JPI is the most complicated. A detailed discussion of its functionality spans several chapters and includes memory, interrupts, drivers used by the JPI, and the microkernel.

The JavaOS Platform Interface

The JPI defines the coupling between the microkernel and the JavaOS Runtime Environment. The JPI facilitates the easy replacement of the microkernel layer because both native and Java software in the runtime rely completely on the JPI to access native functions of the microkernel.

Each implementation of the JPI is microkernel-specific. A simple implementation binds the runtime to the microkernel statically (that is, with a linker) at build time. The benefits of such a simple binding are twofold. First, each microkernel service is just a function call away from the runtime so that the overhead of calling the microkernel from the runtime is low. Second, the runtime and microkernel both run in the CPU's privileged, supervisor-execution mode, simplifying the kernel.

A more complex but correspondingly more flexible binding is possible as well. In this binding, the runtime executes in user mode and then enters into supervisor mode each time the runtime calls the microkernel. The mechanism to enter and exit supervisor mode is CPU-specific, frequently a TRAP instruction.

A user-mode runtime might be necessary when hosting a parallel runtime environment, such as a UNIX variant, on the same microkernel. In such an environment, the JavaOS Runtime Environment can be treated as just another user-mode process for execution by the microkernel.

The current release of JavaOS uses a statically bound, supervisor-mode runtime. Chapters 6, 7, and 8 discuss the JPI in detail.

The Microkernel

The JavaOS microkernel resides between the two lowest levels of JavaOS: the booter and the runtime. The microkernel is a small component of native code that provides services to the runtime through the JPI, including:

- Paging
- Threads
- Interrupts
- Monitors
- Exceptions
- Timers

Think of the microkernel as an optimized host OS, consisting only of the lowest-level primitives that cannot be efficiently implemented in the Java programming language. Chapter 9 explains the microkernel in detail.

The Booter

The booter is the lowest layer of JavaOS and, like the microkernel, is written entirely in native code. The booter loads JavaOS into executable memory and activates the microkernel. Once booted, JavaOS can execute out of either ROM or RAM.

JavaOS can boot from network, ROM, RAM, CD-ROM, floppy, or hard disk devices. The JavaOS Boot Interface (JBI) provides a standard interface for booting, regardless of the boot device. The JBI is a bidirectional interface composed of a single function that transfers control to the microkernel, plus functions to return information about installed devices and to assist the microkernel with managing memory. If multiple CPUs exist, the system boots on a single CPU first. Only after the microkernel activates are additional CPUs utilized. Chapter 10 describes the booter in detail.

1.6   Summary

JavaOS is a new operating system designed from the ground up to host the JDK and Java applications. JavaOS is itself written largely in the Java programming language but actually contains three types of code: native (C and assembler), hardware-independent and platform-independent. JavaOS executes software locally, on the client, but supports the remote or local storage of applications, operating system, and data files. The JavaOS Runtime Environment includes the standard Java Runtime Environment found in the JDK—the Java Virtual Machine, garbage collector, class loader, and core classes. It also includes a collection of JDK hosting classes, device drivers, and system services—the core of true operating systems.

The most important system services of JavaOS are the database, the event system, the service loader, and device drivers. JavaOS relies on a microkernel for the more basic OS functionality, including threads, interrupts, monitors, low-level memory management, and JVM system functions. A layer called the JavaOS Platform Interface abstracts the microkernel from the rest of the JavaOS Runtime Environment so that the runtime can be ported to a variety of microkernels. A native-code booter is responsible for getting the OS up and running.

The end result is an operating system that is highly integrated, yet manageable, secure, and scalable. Because it is designed for different platforms, JavaOS can be used to host the complete (Business) JDK, the Personal JDK (a subset of the Business JDK), or even the smallest JDK subset, called Embedded JDK.

Chapter 2
The Database

The JavaOS System Database, also called the JSD or just "the database," provides storage and retrieval of configuration information for Java software components. Initially, the JSD was designed for JavaOS, but as the need for configuration support on all Java platforms grows, the JSD may be used independently for the purpose.[1]

2.1 Current JDK Configuration Support

The Java Development Kit (JDK) release 1.1 provides configuration support using a simple mechanism called *system properties*. Table 2.1 lists a few of the JDK's standard system properties.

Properties, consisting of a name-value pair, provide software components (applets, applications, beans, and so on) with information about the capabilities and configuration of the platform. As the JDK increases in complexity and reaches increasingly diverse markets, more formal and full-featured configuration support becomes necessary. That's where the JSD comes into play.

2.2 Configuration Support with the JSD

The JSD manages the storage and retrieval of complex configuration information on various Java platforms. Since the JSD is platform-independent, it can be hosted

---

1. The JSD is currently used in a new point of sale (POS) device driver and application standard called JavaPOS software. The JavaPOS software standard is fully described at the following website: http://www.javapos.com. When paired with the JSL and Java Comm API, the JSD enables complete platform-independent POS device drivers and applications.

TABLE **2.1**   Standard Java Properties

Property Name	Property Value
java.version	Version number
java.vendor	Vender name string
java.vendor.url	URL to vendor home page
java.home	Java installation directory
java.class.version	Class version number
java.class.path	Java classpath
os.name	Operating system name
os.arch	Operating system architecture
os.version	Operating system version
file.separator	File separator ("/" on Unix)
path.separator	Path separator (":" on Unix)
line.separator	Line separator ("\n" on Unix)
user.name	User's account name
user.home	User's home directory
user.dir	User's current working directory

on many operating systems, not just JavaOS. Configuration information describes application-specific settings and also includes information on which devices are present on a platform and which software components to install for a user or group of users.

The database is populated (filled with configuration data) during platform initialization. More configuration data is added (and possibly removed) after the operating system (OS) boots. As Figure 2.1 illustrates, the JSD provides a *population interface* for adding configuration data from files, the network, the host OS, applications, and drivers.

2.2.1   Population Methods

A variety of sources can populate the JSD. The set of sources used at any one time depends on the platform's capabilities and usage patterns. The interface Tree-Populator is an API used to fill a hierarchical set of entries (or *tree*) from an outside source such as a file or a PROM.

```
public interface TreePopulator {...}
```

A large amount of the information in the database does not survive across runtime sessions; it is *transient*. Other information in the database persists across runtime sessions. When information is transient, it must be repopulated from its source into the database every time JavaOS boots. For example, the database is

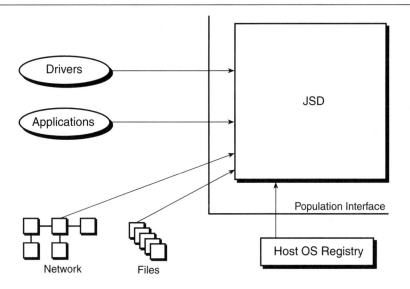

FIGURE 2.1 *JSD Population*

repopulated with information about which devices are installed on the platform every time JavaOS boots. Once the database is populated, changes to the configuration information at the source must be reflected in the database to keep it coherent. Changes to the underlying source data result in the database being refreshed with the new configuration information. Each update to the database in turn results in an event produced to alert applications or system software that the configuration has changed.

For example, if a device is dynamically added to the system after the database is populated with boot device information, the JSD generates an event that activates the discovery of the device driver responsible for the new device. The steps are as follows:

1. An OS component discovers a new device.

2. A device entry is added to the JSD.

3. The JSD produces a configuration change event.

At this point, the OS reacts to the event to find a device driver to manage the new device.[2]

---

2. The JSD is separate and different from Java's network-naming interface, the Java Naming and Directory Interface (JNDI). The JSD is a generic configuration repository; the JNDI abstracts various network naming services, such as Lightweight Directory Access Protocol (LDAP).

2.2.2   Client and Server Components

The JSD uses a split design. One part of the database resides on the server and acts as a proxy for the storage of information that persists across boot sessions as well as a central administration point for all clients connected to the server.

Another part of the database resides on each client and represents the state of the client at any point in time. For example, the server stores settings that specify the software components to load for a particular client, machine group, user, and user group. The server's database contents are managed by the JavaOS Configuration Tool (JCT). The JCT is an applet that allows a system administrator to view and edit the configuration of a single machine, a group of machines (platform), user, or group of users.

The client's database stores settings for the software components that are actually loaded on a client or that are available to a client for loading.

Five general types of settings are possible. They are:

- Settings for a particular machine platform, such as a JavaStation™ network computer.
- Settings for a specific machine instance.
- Settings for a particular group of machines, such as all machines in the purchasing department.
- Settings for a group of users, such as all users on the third floor.
- Settings for a specific user.

Setting Coalescing

For a particular client session, settings from the different categories can conflict. For example, the machine platform settings might specify the loading of a particular print driver by default, but a specific machine might require a different print driver. The settings for a group of users might specify the loading of a particular spreadsheet program when a user from that group logs on, but a specific user from that group might require a different spreadsheet program. A mechanism is required for prioritizing conflicting settings from the different categories. This mechanism is called *coalescing*.

Coalescing occurs at two points during a JavaOS session. The first point occurs during booting. This is when conflicts arise between machine-platform, machine-group, and machine-specific settings. Machine-specific settings have the highest priority and override machine-group and machine-platform, and machine-platform settings override the machine-group settings.

Second, coalescing occurs when a user logs on. Then, conflicts resolve between user group and user-specific settings. User-specific settings have the highest priority and override user-group settings. User settings of any type override machine settings of any type.

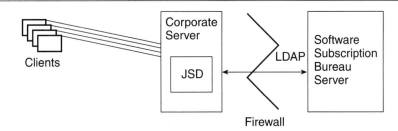

FIGURE 2.2 *Split Database Architecture*

2.2.3 Three-Tier Computing Architecture

You have read how the database is split into two parts, one on the client and one on the server. It actually is possible to split the database three ways: a client part and two parts on different servers, one server holding machine-configuration settings, the other server holding client-configuration settings.

The split database design allows for the implementation of a three-tier subscription-based computing architecture. This architecture, illustrated in Figure 2.2, consists of multiple client machines, a server machine, and a second server belonging to a software subscription service, such as an LDAP server.

The corporate server connects to a server provided by a subscription service, such as an Internet Service Provider. The subscription service hosts all the Java software required by the corporation, including device drivers. The JSD on the corporate server contains a description of the complete set of Java software required by the clients in the corporation. The subscription service automatically loads all this software onto the corporate server (the corporate server acts rather like a proxy server for Java software), and bug fixes and upgrades automatically replace any dated software on the corporate server. Whenever a client boots, the client loads the latest Java software automatically from the corporate server, but only the components the client needs to do the job (as specified in the server JSD).

The corporate IT department never has to become involved in upgrading clients or distributing bug fixes. In fact, it does not need to install any Java software on the corporate server. All IT needs to do is configure the server JSD with the settings for each client. The Java software automatically loads from the subscription server, and upgrades and bug fixes are automatic as well.

2.3 Entries in the Database

The JSD is a collection of named objects, called *entries*, organized as a tree. Each database entry is uniquely identified by a *pathname*, composed of the names of all entries preceding it in the tree hierarchies. Entries can represent files, applications, users, devices, public interfaces, or just about anything else. Entries can have one or more associated properties, each consisting of a name-value pair.

For example, a device entry has a property list describing the memory buffers and interrupt vectors used by the device. A property value might contain a reference to a Java programming language object and, if made persistent, might contain the object itself. For example, an entry representing a device driver contains a reference to the entry for the driver's device.

2.3.1   Entry Interface

The JSD provides an `Entry` interface for creating, reading, changing, and deleting entry properties.

```
public interface Entry {...}
```

Figure 2.3 shows the database entry class hierarchy. Alias, persistent entries, and namespace entries will be described later in the chapter. All entry classes implement the `Entry` interface.

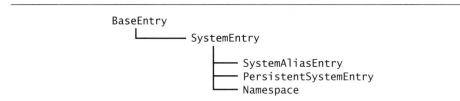

FIGURE 2.3   *Database Entry Class Hierarchy*

2.3.2   Properties

Zero or more properties may be associated with an entry. A property is comprised of a name (`java.lang.String`) and a value (`java.lang.Object`). Methods are provided in the `Entry` interface to add, change, delete, and retrieve properties. Property names also may be enumerated to discover all those present.

No further structure is applied to properties. The name and actual type of the value are strictly up to the user of the property. The JSD supports an implicit Boolean property. If a property is added and no value is provided, the property is considered a Boolean value. Its presence denotes a true value and its absence indicates a value of false.

While the `BaseEntry` class does not itself implement properties, it does implement the public methods used to access and manipulate properties. These methods perform the proper transaction/locking protocol and then invoke the subclass API to access properties.

Methods are provided to add, remove, and change properties. A change occurs when an existing property is assigned a value.

Reading Properties

Invoking the getPropertyCount() method returns the number of properties associated with the entry. The getPropertyNames() method returns a java.util.Enumeration whereby all property names associated with the entry can be enumerated. Given a property name, its value is obtained by the getPropertyValue() method.

Adding Properties and Changing Their Values

The addProperty() method adds a new property or modifies an existing one. If the name of the property to be added does not already exist, one is created and the provided value is associated with the new property name.

If the entry is in the published state, an EntryPropertyInsertEvent is produced for interested consumers. A null Object reference is returned by addProperty(), indicating a new property.

If the property name already exists for the entry, the new value is associated with it, and for published entries an EntryPropertyValueChangeEvent is produced. In this case addProperty() returns the reference of the previous value object.

Removing Properties

A property is removed from an entry using the removeProperty() method. When a property is removed, an EntryPropertyRemoveEvent is produced for published entries. The reference to the value of the removed property is returned.

2.3.3   Entry States

An entry in the JSD is always in one of three states: drafted, published, or archived. The initial construction of entries occurs in a *drafted* state. An entry in the drafted state exists inside the Java language object heap but it is not yet part of the database. Two standard entry object definitions are defined, one for transient entries, another for persistent entries:

```
public class SystemEntry implements Entry {...}
public class PersistentSystemEntry extends SystemEntry {...}
```

An entry is created (drafted) like any other object, using a public constructor:

```
SystemEntry sample = new SystemEntry("SampleName");
```

Because a drafted entry is not a part of the JSD, it can be modified or deleted without causing the generation of a JSD event. More information is available on events in Chapter 3.

Once inserted into the database, an entry enters the *published* state. Interested software components can locate an entry once it is published using its name, properties, or both as search criteria, or by receiving an insertion event.

When a new entry is published, the JSD generates an insertion event that is sent to software components interested in investigating new entries. Such software components are called insertion event listeners. The JSD also might notify interested listeners that the newly published entry has certain properties. If removed from the database, a published entry returns to the drafted state. The virtual machine then either discards and collects the entry or prepares it to enter the third state, the archived state. Removing an entry generates an event so that interested listeners can be notified of the removal. Chapter 3 explains JavaOS's event mechanism in greater detail.

A process known as *serialization* prepares an entry for the *archived* state. Java software language serialization converts an object into a stream of bytes, which then can be persistently stored for later reconstruction. The capability to store and retrieve objects is essential to building all but the more transient applications. For objects to be properly retrieved, their serialized format must contain sufficient information for reconstruction.

Archived entries are stored for future use in a persistent storage location, such as a file, or as an LDAP accessible directory service on the server. The JSD does not play a role in how entries are actually stored: It merely enables them to be stored. Nor does the JSD specify that serialization must be the archiving mechanism used. Thus, another method, such as a simple configuration file on the server, can be used to store persistent portions of the database. No event generates when an entry is archived.

State Transitions

Figure 2.4 illustrates the state transitions an entry may undergo during its lifetime. The numbered transitions are defined as:

1. Entry is constructed.
2. Entry is inserted under a published parent entry. An `EntryInsertEvent` is generated.
3. Published child entry is disconnected from (published) parent. An `EntryDisconnectEvent` is generated.
4. Published entry is removed.
5. Drafted entry is removed.

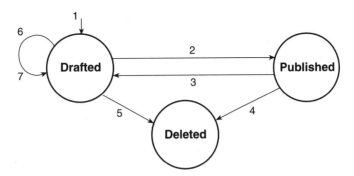

FIGURE 2.4 *Entry State Transitions*

---

6. Drafted entry is inserted under a drafted parent entry.
7. Drafted child entry is disconnected from (drafted) parent.

2.4   JSD Organization

The JSD is organized as a tree of entries. Every entry in the tree descends from a single entry known as the *superroot*, which is created and initialized when the database is initialized. The name of the superroot is "/".

An entry can stand alone or it can serve as the parent of one or more descendant entries, known as *children* or *child entries*. Every entry is limited to a single parent but can have any number of child entries. Children are ordered from left to right. The leftmost (least recently added) child of a parent entry is designated as the first child and the rightmost as the last child. All the children of a parent entry are siblings with respect to one another. All children at a given depth in the tree represent a logical level in the tree. Every entry contains links to its parent, its siblings, and its children. Figure 2.5 illustrates a two-level database tree.

Entries are objects that implement a standard `Entry` interface with methods to identify the entry, its properties, and its neighbors. The `Entry` interface includes methods to do the following:

* Add entry properties
* Retrieve a pathname for the entry
* Disconnect an entry from its parent entry
* Get a child entry, the number of children for an entry, and an enumeration of the children of an entry
* Get the entry's parent

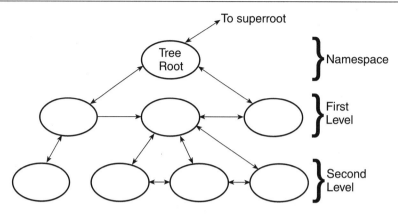

FIGURE 2.5   *Two-level Database Tree*

- Get a property name or value from an entry
- Get a count of an entry's properties
- Check if an entry has a property with a particular name
- Remove a property or child of an entry
- Print an entry
- Check the entry state (published, drafted, or archived)

The JSD database is divided into *namespaces*, which are subtrees of related entries. Namespaces are always direct descendants of the superroot. When the JavaOS Runtime Environment starts, a number of standard namespaces result. Section 2.5 describes the standard namespaces. Namespace entries are instances of the Namespace class and extended class of SystemEntry.

Entries within a given namespace share common characteristics. One namespace might contain entries for all devices and buses on the platform, while another might consist of entries describing a preference or attribute of users of the system.

A default *namespace manager* manages each namespace. The namespace manager controls how entries are created, added, accessed, removed, and updated for a particular namespace. When an entry is published, it inherits its parent's namespace manager by default. For example, the Device namespace manager oversees the Device namespace (one of the standard namespaces you will learn about shortly). When a physical or logical device is discovered at startup time, a device entry is created and assigned the default Device namespace manager. Once a driver is discovered for the device, the driver is made the service for the device entry. Once the driver service matches with a device, the JSL loads the service on demand.

The namespace manager defines the format and organization of entries within a namespace. Standard namespaces support standard entry formats. Nonstandard subtrees of a namespace begin with an entry named using the following naming format:

```
com.uniquename
org.uniquename
edu.uniquename
```

Figure 2.6 illustrates how a standard namespace can descend into nonstandard subtrees.

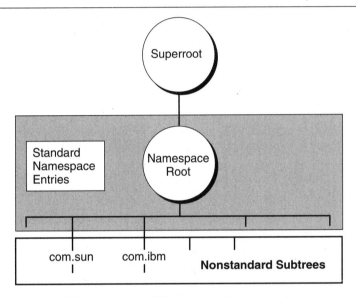

FIGURE 2.6 *Standard Namespace and Nonstandard Subtrees*

2.5   Standard Namespaces

When the JavaOS Runtime Environment starts, it creates six standard namespaces within the database. Standard namespace managers are provided for each of the namespaces. Nonstandard namespaces also be may created by a particular implementation, in which case a nonstandard namespace manager also must be provided. Figure 2.7 illustrates these standard namespaces.

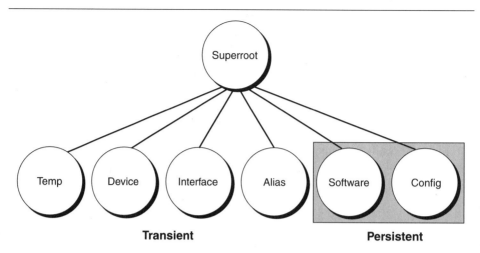

FIGURE 2.7   *Standard Namespaces*

2.5.1   Temp Namespace

The first standard namespace is the Temp namespace. It is available as temporary storage for both application and system software settings. As an example of Temp use, consider the JavaOS Service Loader (JSL). Each time the JSL starts a service, an entry that tracks each instantiation of the service is added to the Temp namespace. Chapter 4 describes the JSL. Temp entries are transient. Once the runtime is shut down, all entries in this namespace are lost.

Initially, the Temp namespace contains no entries other than the namespace root itself. To avoid collisions among temporary namespace users, each software component using this namespace must add its own subtree root entry and operate beneath this root.

2.5.2   Device Namespace

The second standard namespace is the Device namespace. The Device namespace contains the set of devices available to the local platform. The Device namespace entries are transient, and the Device namespace contains no nonstandard entries.

The structure of the Device namespace reflects the physical connectivity between buses and devices on the platform. The root of the Device namespace is named "Device." The one and only immediate child of Device is an entry representing the system CPU. If the system has multiple CPUs, a single entry represents them all, a situation that might change in a future release. The children of the CPU entry represent either system buses or devices residing on the CPU's address bus.

The children of bus entries are entries for all of the devices connected to the bus, which can include other buses. Because devices do not connect to the platform through other devices, the leaf entries (those entries without children) of the Device namespace always represent devices. A bus entry is a leaf only if no devices are connected to the bus; otherwise, the bus entry is the parent of one or more child entries representing connected devices.

Sometimes a bus entry is the parent of another bus entry. This happens when a device (a SCSI adaptor for instance) is used to bridge to another bus. A bus bridge entry becomes the parent of the devices it connects. Figure 2.8 illustrates the Device namespace for a hypothetical platform consisting of a PCI bus with a bridged SCSI bus.

Physical devices and buses are not the only entries present in the Device namespace. Logical devices—a RAMDisk device (a piece of code emulating a hard disk in RAM)—also appears here, directly connected to the CPU address bus.

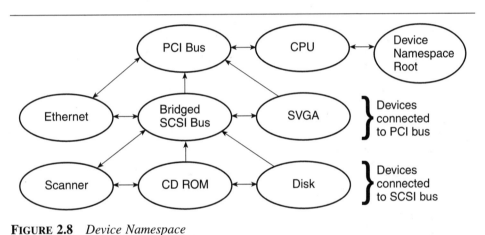

FIGURE 2.8   *Device Namespace*

2.5.3   Interface Namespace

The third standard namespace is the Interface namespace. The Interface namespace contains entries that reference services that implement public Java programming language interfaces. All entries in the Interface namespace are transient.

To understand how the Interface namespace works, consider a serial mouse driver declared as follows:

```
public class xyzMouseDriver implements SerialMouse {...}
```

The SerialMouse interface, in turn, extends the SerialDevice interface.

```
public interface SerialMouse extends SerialDevice {...}
```

Finally, `SerialDevice` extends the generic `Device` interface.

```
public interface SerialDevice extends Device {...}
```

You will learn more about the `Device` interface and how device drivers are created in Chapter 6. For now, make note of the interface hierarchy of the hypothetical mouse driver and compare it with Figure 2.9. This figure illustrates how the driver is represented with an entry in the Interface namespace, and how the entry in the namespace corresponds to the interface hierarchy implemented by the driver.

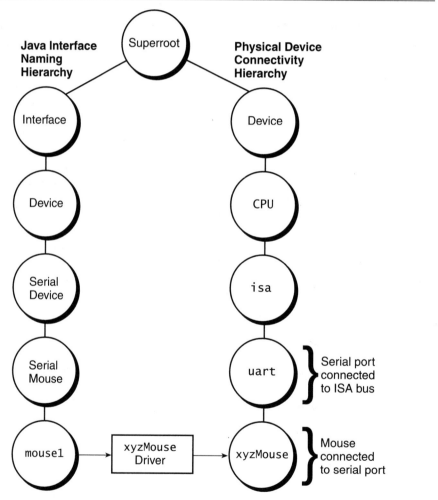

FIGURE 2.9   *Interface Entry for a Mouse Driver*

The process of inserting an `Interface` entry in the JSD is called "advertising the interface." Some interfaces advertise when a service is added to the software namespace; others when a service is matched to a device. The JSL automatically advertises a `service` interface when the service is added to the *Software namespace*.

To locate services implementing the desired functionality, applications, applets, beans, and the OS itself search for advertised interfaces in the Interface namespace. When a service is added to the software namespace, and as devices are discovered and drivers are assigned to the devices, JavaOS notes which interfaces the driver implements. The driver is provided with one or more entries in the Interface namespace for each interface it implements. There is not a one-to-one correspondence between `Interface` and `Device` entries. This is because a single driver may implement more than one interface. For example, a serial device driver might implement `SerialDevice` (for controlling serial devices) as well as `PowerMonitor` (for power management).

Creating a namespace for the interfaces implemented by device drivers enables applications and system services to search for interfaces compatible with the type of I/O they wish to perform, without knowledge of the underlying hardware or driver. Think of device drivers as blocks of code that communicate with higher levels of the system above and with devices and buses below. Drivers implement `Device` interfaces above to communicate with higher levels of the system. Only the `Device` interfaces above the driver are published in the Interface namespace; the names of interfaces below the driver are not. Thus, by querying the Interface namespace, it is possible to discover which device interfaces a driver supports. However, you cannot discover which buses the driver communicates with in this manner.

2.5.4 Alias Namespace

The fourth standard namespace is the Alias namespace. Alias entries reference entries in the Interface namespace and provide friendly naming schemes. For example, an entry in the Alias namespace named `/Alias/system/DefaultPrinter` could refer to the device driver entry `/interface/device/printer/hpInkJet#1` in the Interface namespace. Entries in the Alias namespace are transient.

An alias holds a reference to another entry. It can maintain its own properties, separate from the aliased Interface entry. The aliased entry reference can be obtained using the `SystemAliasEntry getAliasedEntry()` method. This value is immutable and is set at alias construction time. It is possible to construct an alias that does not reference another entry, which only serves as part of the Alias namespace hierarchy. For example, the root Alias namespace entry `/Alias` is an instance of `SystemAliasEntry`, but it does not alias another entry. It only serves as a vehicle for supporting children, which may or may not alias other entries.

An alias may end up referring to a deleted entry when the aliased entry is removed. In this case, the aliased entry is not garbage-collected. Thus, aliases should not be used to reference dynamic entries unless the alias itself is deleted as well.

Multiple aliases may refer to a single entry. However, this does not mean that each alias is a parent of the referenced entry. In fact, no reference is maintained by the aliased entry back to an alias. If the aliased entry is modified in any way, either directly or by way of a property-related method call made on the alias, the associated event is generated with a filter string that names the entry using its natural parent hierarchy. No other events are produced on behalf of the alias itself.

2.5.5 Software Namespace

The fifth standard namespace is the Software namespace, containing an entry for each installed software component. The Software namespace holds the software for only one client (single user, single machine) and contains the client's coalesced view of the Config namespace, described in the next section.

The code for the components is not installed in the Software namespace; instead, a "business card" stores the software description and the loading instructions. For more information on software business cards, see Chapter 4. Software namespace entries are persistent.

The Software namespace exists only on the client and is backed by the Config namespace on the server. The Software namespace can contain both standard and nonstandard formatted entries. Within the Software namespace are subtrees for public software components, virtual devices, virtual machine properties, systems services, and applications. Each of these standard subtrees is divided into standard and nonstandard entries. Figure 2.10 shows the standard Software namespace entries.

The Devices subtree contains entries for devices that cannot be discovered dynamically, such as ISA-bus devices. The *Public* subtree contains standard Java platform information and any other information that a vendor wishes to advertise as public.

2.5.6 Config Namespace

The sixth standard namespace is the Config namespace. The Config namespace maintains client configuration information and contains information about all clients and users. This namespace typically is created and stored on servers, not clients. The Config namespace is persistent. Figure 2.11 depicts the standard subtrees of the Config namespace.

The User subtree contains entries describing the services to load for particular users of the network, and the Machine subtree contains entries describing machines on the network. During a client's booting process, both User and

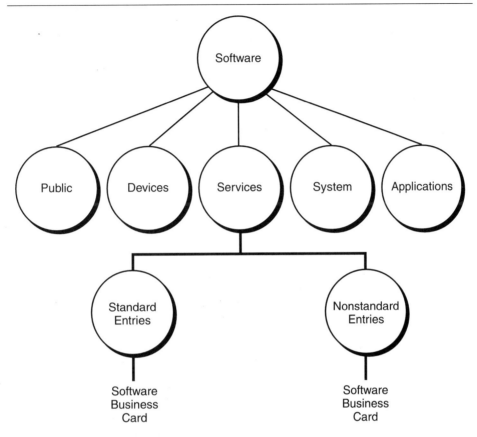

FIGURE 2.10 *Standard Software Namespace Entries*

Machine entries are accessed to dynamically build a client's Software namespace, installing a "personality" on the client. Once the client has booted and is ready to handle a login, the User subtree configuration information comes into play. A user's service and application business cards download into the client's Software namespace.

At login time, the User entries come into play to specify software components and settings to load for the user who is logging in. Device drivers to support the components loaded for the user also might load. By default, a client machine cannot provide access to a particular device (for example, a color printer), but privileged users or groups of users might be given permission to load the color print driver, making the device functional from that machine. When a user logs off, the related services unload and the client returns to the boot-time default state specified for that machine, waiting for the next user. A machine can support only a single user at any one time.

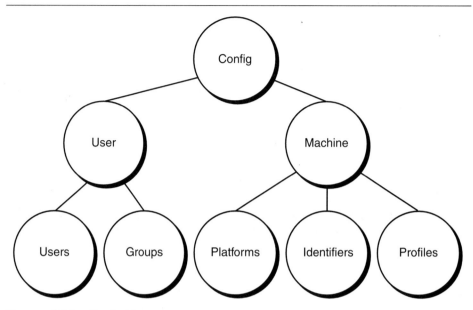

FIGURE 2.11   *Config Namespace*

The standard namespace entries for the User and Machine trees are Users and Groups.

The Users subtree stores an entry for each loadable service applicable to an individual user. The Groups subtree stores an entry for each loadable service applicable to every user belonging to a particular group. The entries in these subtrees pertain to the services to load once the user has successfully logged in; these services are unloaded when the user logs off. The standard subtrees for the Machine tree are Platforms, Identifiers, and Profiles.

- **Platforms** The Platforms subtree defines entries that describe the common characteristics of a family of clients. For example, the Platform entry `JavaStation` defines services and applications to load for all JavaStation™ network computers.

- **Identifiers** The Identifiers subtree stores the entries that describe the software that is specific to a particular client. A hardware-unique identifier, the Media Access Control (MAC) address, identifies a particular client machine.

- **Profiles** The Profiles subtree contains entries that describe the current overall software personality for a particular client. The current software personality

is the composite of the settings in effect for a particular machine at a given
point in time.

Figure 2.12 illustrates a populated Config namespace. Each rectangle in the
figure represents a business card (a collection of properties) for a particular software component to load.

When user Joe logs in, the server locates Joe's entry in the User subtree. The
software components to load for Joe include his personal software components
and the software components for all users in the Finance group to which Joe
belongs. The group components are installed first, followed by the individual
components.

In Figure 2.12, a unique identifier enables the server to locate a particular client
machine in the Identifiers subtree. In this case, the unique ID for the machine Joe logged
on to is the MAC address of `08:00:20:87:be:a7`. Software components specific
to that machine are located, and since the machine is part of the `JavaStation-2`
platform, additional components for that platform load as well. The platform components load first, followed by the machine-specific components.

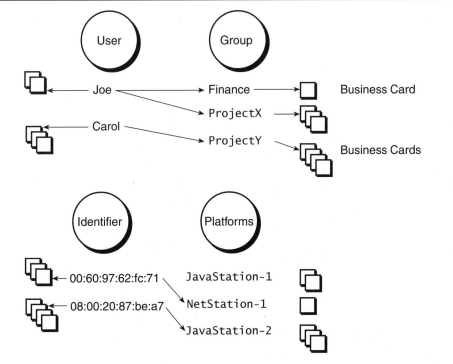

FIGURE 2.12 *A Populated Config Namespace*

2.6   Entry Format

Every entry in the database must implement the `Entry` interface. The `BaseEntry` and `SystemEntry` base classes define the most common, general-purpose entry behavior.

Each entry stores (as properties) the entry's name, status, lock, manager, and references to its neighbor entries. Figure 2.13 shows a typical system database entry.

The entry *name* is a `java.lang.String` object, and can contain any unicode characters except for the pathname component separator character. There are no other character restrictions, but the name cannot be a null reference or empty string, and the name must be unique among all of the siblings of the parent under which the entry resides.

The `SystemEntry` class defines an additional naming restriction. The pathname component separator character ("/") cannot be used in the name string.

Status stores the state of the entry. An entry has three states: drafted, published, and archived.

The *parent entry* is a reference to the entry's anchor-point entry, under which the entry was inserted. Each entry can have one parent at most.

The *child entry* refers to the leftmost (oldest) entry inserted under the parent. Additional children are accessed using the sibling pointers of the children.

Sibling entry links are references to the other children sharing the same parent entry.

A reader-writer *lock* mechanism is provided (`SystemDatabaseLock`) so that an entry can be inspected or modified without interference. The Java programming language monitor mechanism (`synchronized` keyword) provides for an object to be exclusively locked within the scope of the synchronized keyword (code block or entire method). However, the database entry lock allows for multiple sequential method calls to be made while the entry is locked. It also allows for multiple concurrent readers.

```
Name (String)
Status (Drafted, Published, Achieved)
Parent Entry Link
Sibling Entry Links
Child Entry Link
Lock
Manager
Generation Number
```

+

Entry-Specific Properties

FIGURE 2.13 *Entry Anatomy*

Locks can be acquired for either shared or exclusive access. The methods defined in `TransactionFactory` (implemented by `BaseEntry`) determine the entry lock mode to use. Multiple shared transactions may access the same lock simultaneously. Once an exclusive transaction acquires a lock, all other transactions are blocked until the lock is released.

The *entry manager is* a software component that oversees each entry in the database. The entry manager is responsible for inserting and removing the entry, and modifying entry properties. For example, device drivers typically are the entry managers for entries in the Device namespace. By default, an entry inherits the manager of its parent when it is inserted into the database. However, the manager can be changed using the `Entry` interface method `setManager()`. When a Device entry is matched with a driver, its manager changes from the default inherited through its parent to the driver. The namespace root entry's manager is the default entry manager established when the namespace first creates.

The entry *generation number* is a monotonically increasing integer data type that increments whenever the entry is changed, regardless of the status of the entry. This provides a tracking mechanism for simple coherency schemes.

An entry changes whenever it is inserted or removed from the database, or when any property additions, changes, or deletions are made.

An entry can have any number of *properties*. A property is identified by a name (a `String` object), and its value is a reference to an object. The `Entry` interface provides methods to add, remove, and change properties. If the value object itself changes in some manner (for example, bytes changed in a byte array) rather than the property value (the reference), the database is unable to detect the change. It is the responsibility of the entity making such a change to notify interested listeners by assigning the same property name and value to the entry again. In this way, the generation number is incremented and an event produced.

2.7 Persistent Entries

A key responsibility of a namespace manager is the management of an entry's persistence. Of the seven standard namespaces, only the Software and Config namespaces contain persistent entries. Persistent entries need not be stored on the client. Typically, they persist on the server and are merely downloaded to the client at boot time. The JSD's default entry class, `SystemEntry`, is not persistent. Namespace managers wishing to make entries persistent use a subclass of `SystemEntry` called `PersistentSystemEntry`.

Configuration entries on the server are made persistent using a `Persistent-SystemEntry` that performs read/write operations to and from a datastore, such as a file or a directory service accessed by LDAP. Figure 2.14 shows the connection

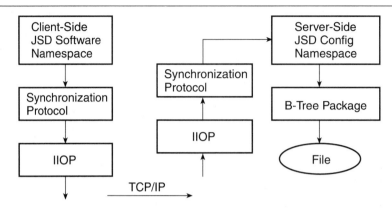

FIGURE 2.14   *Persistent Configuration Entries on Server*

between the client-side JSD and the persistent configuration entries available on the server.

Software namespace persistence is currently accomplished using InterORB Operability Protocol (IIOP) and a JSD entry-synchronization protocol. Any number of other protocols, such as Hypertext Transfer Protocol (HTTP) or Remote Method Invocation (RMI), could be used just as easily to connect the client's Software namespace to both the server's Config namespace and the associated persistent storage found on the server.

2.8   Trees

Any arbitrary database entry can be designated as the root of a database subtree. These root entries implement the Tree interface. All descendants of the root are part of the tree. Figure 2.15 shows the attributes of a typical system database tree.

A tree is named after and referenced by the name of its root entry. Entries in the tree can be referenced by a pathname that is relative either to the root of the tree or to a designated *current entry* in the tree. Pathnames starting with a / name

```
Root Entry
Current Entry
Transaction Lock
Tree Populator
Find and New
```

FIGURE 2.15   *Database Tree Attributes*

an entry relative to the tree root. All other pathname forms identify entries relative to the current entry. The Tree interface provides methods to get and set the current entry.

2.8.1 Transaction Lock

A transaction defines a set of entries and is the means by which one or more related entries in the JSD can be locked and accessed in an atomic manner. Access to the set is defined to be either shared or exclusive. In the latter case, only a single transaction can be used to access the entry set. All others will block until the set becomes available.

The JSD transaction model operates on a subtree of the database. A subtree is illustrated by the shaded entries in Figure 2.16. The subtree is defined by a root entry and extends throughout the hierarchy of its descendants.

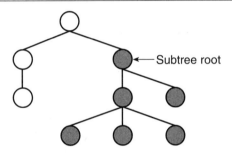

FIGURE 2.16 *Transaction Scope*

A read/write transaction lock (associated with each entry in the subtree) is used to lock the entire tree, which allows coherent transactions to be performed on large sections of the system database. Transactions might be blocked while waiting for the current tree transaction to complete. Blocking time can be limited by setting a maximum time parameter when beginning a transaction.

Transactions are accomplished on trees using a Transaction object. The Transaction object provides commit/abort/rollback functionality for supporting tree-atomic operations. Transactions can be shared or exclusive. A shared transaction allows more than one client to operate on the tree at once. Transactions are especially useful for adding or deleting multiple entries at one time.

2.8.2 Tree Population

The TreePopulator interface provides a general mechanism for populating a tree. This interface supports both simple and complex methods of population. For example, a simple platform such as a phone has a well-known number of fixed devices. There is no need to do device discovery every time the phone boots. An array of strings easily represents the devices in the phone. The TreePopulator interface allows such simple devices to populate sections of the database from a predefined static table of strings. More complex platforms can implement a TreePopulator based on, to a name a few possibilities, OpenBoot firmware, host registries, files, and so on.

TreePopulator includes methods for retrieving the parent or children of an entry, as well as the entry's peers (those entries on the same tree level as the entry). Using TreePopulator it also is possible to retrieve the root entry of the tree, as well as the name or value of any property in an entry of the tree.

The following example shows how a static source, such as a String array class, can populate the database with entries. Other static sources include files and flash memory. In this example, the platform device entries are first defined in a string that is encapsulated into an extended StaticTree class. The StaticTree acts as a container for the static device entry descriptions. The following string is encapsulated in the StaticTree class and describes the devices available on the platform:

```java
public class PlatformServiceStaticTree extends StaticTree {
...
private String[] platformTreeData = {
  "TREE service {",
    "ENTRY javax {",
      "ENTRY comm {",
        "ENTRY CommPort {",
          "PROPERTIES {",
          "bundleFileName = CommPort.jar;",
          "bundleURL = file:/platform/packages/javax/comm/;",
          "bundleType = JAR;",
          "bundleInitClassName = [null:0];",
          "bundleInstanceInfo =
             CommPort,CommPort,javax.comm.CommPort;",

          "matchingName = CommPortIdentifier;",

          "loadsUponConnection = false;",
          "loadsUponMatched = true;",
          "loadsUponDiscovered = false;",
          "}",
        "}",
      "}",
    "}",
    "ENTRY jpos {",
      "ENTRY CashChangerService12 {",
        "PROPERTIES {",
        "DeviceServiceDescription = NCR 24 CashChanger;",
        "DeviceServiceVersion = 1002038;",
        "PhysicalDeviceDescription = NCR.CashChanger.4800;",
```

```
    "PhysicalDeviceName = NCR.CashChanger.4800;",
    "}",
  "}",
  "ENTRY CashDrawerService12 {",
    "PROPERTIES {",
    "DeviceServiceDescription = SUN 24 CashDrawer;",
    "DeviceServiceVersion = 1002038;",
    "PhysicalDeviceDescription = NCR.Drawer.4800;",
    "PhysicalDeviceName = NCR.Drawer.4800;",
    "}",
  "}",................
```

The first entry in the static description is for the platform COM port. It is named CommPort and has the properties associated with the device's business card. You will learn more about business cards in Chapter 4.

For now, just know that the static PROPERTIES for the COM port are used to create an entry in the Software namespace for the COM port. The JSL uses this entry to load the device driver classes that control the port.

The number of devices described in the StaticTree class actually is very large. The example shows only two others—one for the cash changer and one for the drawer. What you are seeing are descriptions of a couple of the devices found in a cash register running JavaOS.

The StaticTree is input to a class implementing the TreePopulator interface, called StaticTreePopulator. This class, in turn, invokes a StaticTreeCompiler class on the StaticTree, and the String in StaticTree is converted into an array of entry objects suitable for storage in the JSD. Each entry object contains a list of properties, each property with its own list of attributes. Figure 2.17 illustrates these relationships.

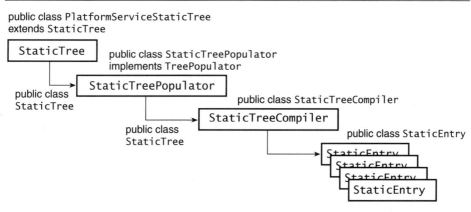

FIGURE 2.17 *Population Using a StaticTree*

2.8.3   Pathnames

The Tree interface defines methods to locate entries within a tree, as well as to add new entries to a tree. Trees are located using a pathname. A tree pathname is a string that identifies an entry in the database. Pathnames are interpreted relative to either the superroot or designated current entry within the database. The syntax rules for pathnames are as follows:

The JSD uses / as the entry name separator, with the superroot named /. Therefore, absolute pathnames always begin with /. Embedded / characters denote a parent-child relationship between the /-separated Entry names. Therefore, *a/b* indicates *b* is the child of *a* in the JSD hierarchy. Multiple, contiguous /'s are interpreted as requests to ascend the hierarchy (rather than the single / descent). In fact, the pathname is a directed walk of the tree. For example, /a/b/c//d directs a "walk" from *a* down to *b,* down to *c,* up to *d* (which must be a sibling of *b*). a/b/c///d would still "walk" from *a* down to *b,* down to *c;* but *d* (two levels up) would be a sibling of *a* rather than of *b* as in the previous example.

Algorithmically, you scan for / characters and count how many contiguous ones you find. If the count is one, you descend. If it's more than one, you ascend "count – 1" levels before continuing the walk.

The character "." also is reserved (as is /) and not allowed in JSD entry names. This restriction is necessary to support easy translation between JSD pathnames and package names (that is, com.sun.javaos). All other characters can be

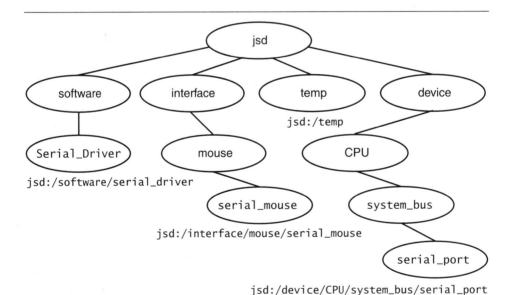

FIGURE 2.18 *Pathname Examples*

used anywhere in the `Entry` names. For instance, `Entry` names can be used that start with numbers or have embedded spaces, and so on.

Also, trailing `/`'s are not legal in pathnames, so *a/b/* is not legal, but *a/b* is valid.

However, the JSD silently trims trailing `/`'s as a convenience to the clients. All "characters" and "pathnames" are formed using unicode strings.

Pathnames are useful for displaying the contents of a namespace. Browsers supporting the Java programming language can be used to graphically display the entries in a namespace if the browser is configured to understand the JSD protocol. The Uniform Resource Locator (URL) `jsd:/Device/x/y/z` requests the browser to display one or more entries in the Device namespace. Also, system properties can be displayed with a URL such as `jsd:/Properties/x/y/z`.

Given the appropriate URL, a database-savvy debugger also can display configuration information.

2.9   Database Events

The JSD generates events to indicate changes to the entries within the database. All database events are descendants of the `SystemDatabaseEvent` base class, which in turn is a subclass of `OSFilteredEvent`. A filtered event allows some events to not be delivered, based on a matching string (a JSD pathname in this case). For more details on events, see Chapter 3, The Event System.

The subclass of `SystemDatabaseEvent` indicates the type of JSD event. For database-change events, the `getEntry()` method of the event object returns a reference to the affected entry object. There are two major JSD event categories:

- Insertion and removal of entries
- Changes to the properties of an entry (adding, removing, or changing a property)

Figure 2.19 shows the database `Event` class hierarchy.

Event listeners for a particular class of event will receive notification not only for events of that type, but also for subclasses of that event type. For example, by listening for an `EntryPropertyEvent`, the listener will receive events of type `EntryPropertyEvent` and all of its subclasses. The listener receives all events pertaining to property changes.

Listeners listening for `SystemDatabaseEvent` receive all database-related events. `Event` class types can be distinguished with the Java programming language `instanceof` operator. `EntryEvent` and all its subclasses contain a reference to the affected entry. `EntryPropertyEvent` and its subclasses can be

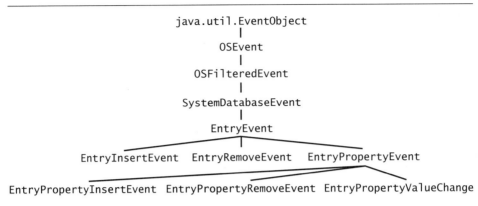

FIGURE 2.19   *JSD Event Class Hierarchy*

queried for the name of the affected property. The previous property value from before the change is available from either `EntryPropertyRemoveEvent` or `EntryPropertyValueChangeEvent`.

The system PCMCIA device manager is a good example of a software component that registers to receive database events. The PCMCIA device manager listens for insertion and removal events from the Device namespace and then loads or unloads the device driver and other components for the device being inserted or removed.

The response to an event by one listener sometimes generates events that require another listener to take action. The insertion of a PCMCIA modem card, for example, prompts the PCMCIA manager to load the driver for the card and to create entries in the Interface namespace for interfaces implemented by the FCM-CIA modem card driver. This action generates more events and that might result in the loading of additional components, such as a dialer applet. See Chapter 3 for more details on the JavaOS event system.

2.10   Database Navigation

The JSD is navigated using either cursors or pathnames. Cursor navigation, provided by the `Cursor` class, enables directional movement relative to the current database entry. A cursor is an object that exists outside of the database, tracking a position in the database and accepting commands to change that position. The *current entry* is the entry pointed to at any moment by a cursor. Any number of cursors can be active at a time, representing many current entries in the database.

Pathname navigation is provided by the findEntry() method defined by the Tree interface. Given a pathname, this method returns a database entry, or null if the path is invalid. In addition, the Query class is provided to perform more complex searches based on entry and property names.

Cursor and pathname navigation are interrelated. A cursor is constructed using a pathname to specify the entry to use as the initial current entry for the cursor. The findEntry() method uses cursors to navigate the database, matching entry names with pathname components to converge on the final named entry.

The Entry interface provides methods for both cursors and pathname navigation. These are the methods neighborEntry(), locate(), and isBasename(). Cursors make use of the neighborEntry() method to move in a direction from the current entry. Defined as final constants in the Cursor class, directions are UP, DOWN, LEFT, and RIGHT. The SystemEntry class, used to create a hierarchical tree of entries, interprets the directions as shown in Figure 2.20.

The locate() method allows an entry to indicate whether it is part of a specified pathname. The entry is part of a pathname when it is the target entry of the pathname, or an entry traversed en route to the target entry. An object of the class LocateResult is provided to locate(). In addition to indicating whether a pathname component matches the entry, the locate() method also updates the pathname by truncating the portion of the path that described the entry to which it was passed. The truncated pathname then can be passed down the tree for testing by children and siblings of the entry. When the pathname is completely truncated, the cursor is positioned on the target entry.

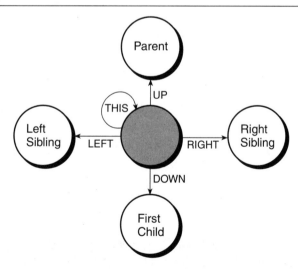

FIGURE 2.20 *Navigation Directions*

2.10.1   Cursors

Cursors accept the following navigation commands: move down, move up, move left, and move right. These commands enable movement from any entry in the database to any other, one entry at a time, according to the meanings assigned in Figure 2.20. Cursors also support a "goto" facility that provides the ability to jump directly to a new location through specification of either a relative or an absolute pathname.

2.10.2   Searching the Database

The JSD defines a Query class that searches the database for one or more entries matching designated criteria. The matching criteria can include the entry name or any property name.

Query objects are constructed using a cursor-and-search criteria. A query provides an enumeration interface to walk through a list of entries matching the criteria. Additional methods to reset and back up the search also are provided.

The scope of a query search can be the current entry, parent, siblings, children, or descendants of the current entry. Like cursors, query objects exist outside the bounds of the database. Each query stores search criteria, search scope, state, and results of the search. Figure 2.21 illustrates the format of a Query object.

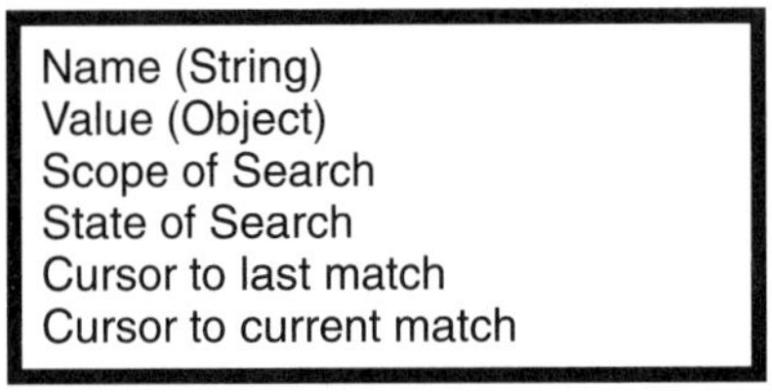

```
Name (String)
Value (Object)
Scope of Search
State of Search
Cursor to last match
Cursor to current match
```

FIGURE 2.21   *Format of a Query*

2.11   Summary

The JavaOS System Database provides storage and retrieval of configuration information for Java software components. The JSD is organized as a tree of entries, each entry describing configuration settings for a component (both software and hardware) of the client. The database is divided into six standard subtrees called Software, Config, Temp, Device, Alias, and Interface. Entries in the database are identified by a pathname, which is just the location of the entry relative to the root of the tree.

The database uses a split design. On the server, the configuration information is stored for each user and client machine on the network. The database on each client is populated from the server at boot time with configuration information about a particular machine, group of machines, and machine platform. At login time, each client database is populated with configuration information about the user who is logging in and the group of users he or she belongs to, if any. The populated database is navigated using `Cursor` objects and searched using `Query` objects.

Chapter 3
The Event System

In both JavaOS and the Java Development Kit (JDK), an event is an object containing information that is exchanged between two objects. When it comes to events, the main difference between JavaOS and the JDK™ lies in how events are routed between the source and destination objects. In the JDK Version 1.2, events are routed using a peer-to-peer mechanism. The source object directly calls a method in the destination object, passing the event to the method.

In JavaOS, events are routed through a central broker. Source and destination objects register with an event manager (the broker), which handles the routing of events from a source to one or more destination objects. As you will see shortly, using a central broker to route events offers many advantages over peer-to-peer routing.

In JavaOS, events play a central role in enabling the secure, reliable, and predictable exchange of information between objects. Events are particularly useful for synchronous and asynchronous I/O between clients and device drivers.

3.1 JDK Event Routing

By way of comparison, we first review the event routing model implemented in the JDK Version 1.2.

Event routing in the JDK is based upon a peer-to-peer model. This means that an object that wants to receive a specific type of event (called a listener for that event type) must search for active objects that can supply that type of event (called sources for that event type) and register with each source to receive events.

Each source must keep a list of all registered listeners for a particular event type and must pass each new event object of that type to each registered listener.

Each source also must provide a mechanism for listeners to remove themselves from the list of objects to receive events. A side effect of this approach is that each event is processed within the listener object on the current thread, unless the listener object requests a thread switch.

JavaOS is a hosting environment for the JDK. This means that at some point, JavaOS events must be converted into JDK events before they are passed up to applications. The reverse is also true. It is the responsibility of the JDK hosting classes (part of the JavaOS Runtime Environment) to perform this event translation function. Figure 3.1 illustrates event routing in the JDK.

The event routing model used by the JDK puts a lot of responsibility on the listener. Not only must the listener search out and register with all event sources for a particular event type, it also must diligently keep watch for additional sources loaded after the initial search. Otherwise, the listener will not register with the newly active source object and will not receive events from it.

The listener also must be a good neighbor and provide a thread switch if the event processing code has high latency. Otherwise, the listener could block the event source from dispatching more events (assuming a single dispatch thread). Unfortunately, despite all the work it must do, the listener does not have any control over the order in which it receives events. As the last listener to register for the event, it might receive the event first, before any other registered listeners (a Last

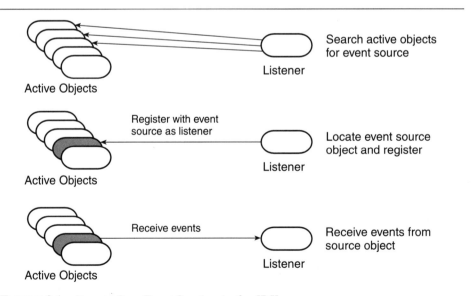

FIGURE 3.1   *Peer-to-Peer Event Routing in the JDK*

In First Out, LIFO, algorithm), or it might receive the event last (a First In First Out, FIFO, algorithm). The order of dispatch is entirely at the discretion of the source class.

The event source does not get off much easier. It must provide queues for each type of event it produces and methods for listeners to register and unregister for events. It also must keep a list of which listeners registered for what event and must call the listener method of all registered listeners for each event type. This could involve establishing multiple threads, one per event type, or possibly even one per event listener.

3.2 JavaOS Event Routing

Unlike the JDK, JavaOS uses a broker to assist in routing events between source and listener objects. Because of this different model, JavaOS has adopted a different terminology than the one used by the JDK to describe event routing. In JavaOS, objects that are the source of events are called *producers*. Objects that listen for events are called *consumers*. The event manager is the code that sits in the middle, acting as the broker. Figure 3.2 illustrates event routing in JavaOS.

All objects that produce events register with the event manager as producers. Also, all objects that consume events register with the event manager as consumers. When an object registers as a producer, it specifies the event types it can produce. Consumers specify the types of events they wish to receive. Thus, the event manager acts as a central repository of information about every object in the

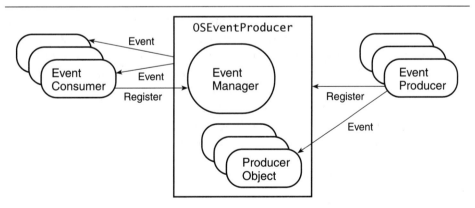

FIGURE 3.2 *JavaOS Event Routing*

system that produces or consumes events, and every type of event they produce or consume.

Using a broker model has several advantages. First, consumers do not have to scan the entire set of active objects to determine which objects produce the types of events in which the consumer is interested. Consumers merely register with the event manager and are automatically routed events from producers of the desired event type. (Consumers wishing to receive events from a specific producer are also supported by the event system.) Consumers can even request that the event manager deliver all event types that are subclasses of the event types for which they register.

Second, new producers can be added at any time and the consumers will not have to rescan the system to find them. When a new producer registers with the event manager, it is automatically connected with any consumers that are already registered for the type of event it produces.

Third, queuing and dispatching of events can be centralized within the event manager. Producers simply pass event objects to the event manager, which is responsible for queuing and dispatching the events.

Fourth, the event manager can perform a thread switch so that the event consumer cannot block the producer.

Finally, consumers can request that the event manager give them priority over certain types of events, in effect moving the consumer to the front of the event queue for that event type.

3.3   Event System Classes

Together, the classes for implementing events, event producers, event consumers, and the event manager make up the JavaOS event system. The `OSEvent` class (`javaos.javax.system.events.OSEvent`) is the base class for all objects exchanged as events. This class contains a reference to the event's producer and specifies how the event should be consumed (more on this later).

To create more specific event types, simply subclass `OSEvent` (or one of its subclasses). `OSEvent` contains methods for returning the event's producer and consumption type (described later on), and for copying the private data of one event to another.

To create an event consumer, a class must implement the `OSEventConsumer` interface. This interface contains methods for returning the types of events to receive, the name of the consumer, returning matching rules, returning an event filter, and a handler method to which the event manager passes event objects.

3.3.1   Consumer Ordering Rules

The OSEventConsumer interface is sufficient for specifying which event types the consumer should receive. But what if the consumer also needs to specify the order in which it receives events, relative to other consumers of the same event types?

In this situation, the consumer should implement the OSEventOrderedConsumer interface. When a consumer implementing this interface is registered with the event manager, the event manager assigns the consumer a default position in the list of consumers receiving the same event. The event manager then calls a method in the OSEventOrderedConsumer interface to query the consumer as to whether this assigned position is acceptable. If the position is not acceptable, the consumer indicates disapproval of the position and the event system might attempt to assign a different position. However, if the position desired by the consumer conflicts with the desired position of an earlier-assigned consumer for the same event type, the new consumer is rejected.

Even generic consumers will be rejected if they conflict with the priority assigned to a prioritized consumer. When a generic consumer registers for an event type, the event manager consults the list of prioritized consumers for events of that type. If a prioritized consumer objects to insertion of the generic consumer, the generic consumer is rejected.

3.3.2   Producer Classes

Event producer objects are created from classes extending the OSEventProducer abstract base class. Producer objects are constructed with a list of the types of events to produce. Notice that unlike consumer objects, producer objects are distinct from the event producer object itself. In other words, to produce events, a producer instantiates a separate producer object and invokes a method on that object specifying the event to produce.

The event can be specified by passing the producer object the actual event to produce or by specifying the type of event (or events) to produce. One producer can produce multiple event types.

Event consumers are merely instances of classes implementing OSEventConsumer; there is no consumer object separate from the event consumer class. Figure 3.2 illustrates these relationships. Notice that each event producer creates a producer object and then passes the events to that object. Consumers are themselves the consumer object.

The event producer can be derived from any class. It does not have to extend OSEventProducer, although the producer object must be an instance of a class extending OSEventProducer.

Why have a producer object that is distinct from the event producer class itself? The advantage is that the producer object can optionally perform a thread switch when the event object is passed to it by the event producer class, before the event passes along to the event manager. The thread switch provides an additional level of isolation between the behavior of the event producer class and consumers of the event. This isolation is especially useful when the event producer class is a device driver or other critical system class.

Again, look carefully at Figure 3.2. Notice the box around the producer objects and the event manager. The box is labeled "OSEventProducer." This box shows how the same class, OSEventProducer, implements the event manager code and the producer objects. The static methods and data of OSEventProducer implement the event manager. The instance methods and data of OSEventProducer implement the producer objects. In this manner, OSEventProducer has some attributes of a centralized event broker (the event manager) and some attributes of a distributed event model (separate producer objects for each event type to produce).

Event producers are any class with an associated OSEventProducer object. Passing an event object to an associated OSEventProducer object causes the event to be queued and dispatched to consumers that have registered for events of that type.

3.4   Registration

Registration is the process of adding an event producer class or an event consumer class to the list of producers and consumers maintained by the event manager. Both producers and consumers must be registered.

3.4.1   Producer Registration

The event manager maintains only a single master list of registered producers, regardless of the type of event or how many types of events are produced. To register as an event producer, a class calls the static register() method of OSEventProducer. This results in placement of the event producer on the master list of event producers. For security, the event producer class can specify whether it can be the only source of events of a particular type. Otherwise, multiple producers can produce the same type of event, and registered consumers for that type will receive them all. To unregister, an event producer must call unRegister(). When a producer is unregistered, all pending events from that producer are purged from the dispatch queue in the event manager.

3.4.2 Consumer Registration

For consumers, the event manager maintains multiple lists. One list is a master list of all registered consumers. In addition to the master list, the event manager maintains one list for each type of event to be consumed. For example, if there are five registered event consumers for three separate types of events, the event manager will maintain four separate lists: one master list with five entries (one for each registered consumer) and one separate list for each event type. To register as a consumer, a class calls the static method subscribeConsumer() in OSEventProducer. The event manager then adds the consumer to the event manager's master consumer list. To unregister a consumer, a class calls unSubscribeConsumer(). The event manager removes the consumer from the master consumer list and unlinks the consumer from any event-type lists.

Looking carefully at Figure 3.2, notice that the arrow labeled "register" between the event producer class and OSEventProducer ends outside the box, not inside it. This detail was added to emphasize the fact that registering as an event producer actually registers the producer object associated with an event producer, not the event producer itself. From the perspective of the event manager, the event comes from the associated producer object, not the event producer. The same is not true for event consumers; they represent the consumer object and register directly with the event manager.

3.4.3 Peer-to-Peer Registration

Suppose that an event consumer wants to receive events from one or more specific producers. In other words, the consumer does not want to register to receive events by type, it wants to receive events from particular producers.

To find a registered producer from which to receive events, the consumer class retrieves an OSEventProducerEnumerator object from the event manager by calling the producers() method. Next, the consumer calls the nextElement() method of this class to retrieve a reference to each producer object in the list. When the consumer locates the producer it wants to work with, it calls the static connectConsumer() method in OSEventProducer with a reference to the producer object. The consumer then will receive events from that producer alone. The consumer can specify whether it wants to be the exclusive consumer of events from that producer. Again, this is useful for security reasons.

In a similar fashion, a registered consumer can be located by first retrieving an OSEventConsumerEnumerator object by calling the consumers() method. When retrieved from the event manager (the static portion of OSEventProducer), this object contains the master list of all registered consumers. References to each consumer in the list are returned using calls to the method `nextElement()`. To enumerate the consumers that are registered to receive a particular type of event from a particular producer object, first obtain a reference to the producer object (using `OSEventProducerEnumerator`), then retrieve an `OSEventConsumerEnumerator` from that producer object. The enumerator will contain a list of consumers that are registered to receive events of a particular type from that particular producer object. In all cases, the enumeration object is only a snapshot of registered producers or consumers. When a new registration occurs, it is not reflected in currently instantiated enumeration objects.

3.4.4   Event Matching Rules

As a result of registration, the event manager will match consumers with producers of events in one of three ways. The first way is to directly match the consumer with events of the exact type specified. This is called exact matching. The second way is to match consumers with the event type specified and with all event objects that are extended types of the type specified. This is called subtype matching. Finally, a consumer can specify that it wants to receive events that match a specified filter, which is a common string specified by both the event and the consumer. With filtered matching, when the event manager receives an event from a producer, it calls the `getFilter()` method of the event object and retrieves the filter string. The event manager then calls the `getFilter()` method of the consumer to retrieve the consumer's specified filter. If the consumer's filter string is present and starts with the event's filter string, the event is sent to the consumer.

Filtered Events

Filtered matching is most useful for consumers that want to receive events from a subtree of the JSD. With filtered matching, a consumer specifies to the event manager a string representing a path to the root of the JSD subtree from which it wants to receive events. Any event generated by an entry of that subtree is sent to the event manager with a filter string that specifies the entry's path in the JSD. The path of entries in the JSD subtree contains a starting substring that includes the root of the subtree, so that all such events are matched with the consumer that specified the subtree root as a filter string.

   The matrix in Figure 3.3 depicts the various consumer and event-filtered matching scenarios.

	Event contains a string	Event contains a null
Consumer contains a string	Conditional. If match, give to the consumer. If no match, no error generated.	No match; error generated to the producer.
Consumer contains a null	Match; give to the consumer.	Match; give to the consumer.

FIGURE 3.3 *Consumer and Event-Filtered Matrix*

3.5 Bidirectional Events

Events are a means of formal information exchange between producers and consumers. As such, events form the basis of many types of inter-class communications. Because much communication is bidirectional (a dialog) as opposed to unidirectional (a monologue), JavaOS supports the concept of response events. Response events are used in situations where the producer of events expects a response back from consumers of the events it produces. Response events are a way for consumers to send events to producers (but only in response to received events). A response event is an object implementing the OSEventResponse interface.

Bidirectional communication is especially useful when performing asynchronous I/O with device drivers. For example, an applet might wish to write data to a network device. The applet creates a producer object, registers with the event manager, then sends data to the driver in the form of an event. The driver consumes the event, writes out the data asynchronously, and then acknowledges that all the data was written by sending a response event back to the applet. The applet then sends more data, and the cycle repeats.

3.6 Types of Consumption

JavaOS supports three main types of event consumption: shared, exclusive, and competitive. Support for the three types is a cooperative effort between the event manager and consumers.

3.6.1   Shared Consumption

Shared consumption is the most common method of event consumption. With shared consumption, the event manager routes events of a particular type to all consumers that have registered for that type. The event manager waits for one consumer to complete its processing of the event before passing the event on to the next registered consumer. Event processing is considered complete when the consumer's event listener method returns. The same event object is passed to all registered consumers. Thus, if one consumer's listener method alters the contents of the event object, the changes are visible to all other consumers that subsequently receive the event.

3.6.2   Exclusive Consumption

Exclusive consumption involves the formation of a one-to-one relationship between a consumer and an event type. All events of a specified type are consumed by a single consumer. It is up to the consumer to specify that it wants the exclusive relationship by identifying to the event manager the event type. When exclusive consumption is specified, any attempt by a later consumer to register for events of that type is rejected.

3.6.3   Competitive Consumption

The final type of event consumption is competitive consumption. Competitive consumption is only available to consumers that have implemented the OSOrderedEventConsumer interface. This interface allows the consumer to specify its priority in the dispatch order when receiving events of a particular type. Unlike shared consumption, in competitive consumption a consumer can halt the dispatch of events to other consumers with a lower priority, in effect preventing those consumers from ever seeing the event. If you recall, in shared consumption the event manager waits until a consumer's listener method returns from processing an event before dispatching the event to the next consumer in the list. With competitive consumption, the event manager also waits for the listener method to return. However, if the listener method returns a special "kill dispatch" value, the event manager will break out from its dispatch loop and the event will not be delivered to any other consumers in the list.

3.7   Threading

The event manager supports several threading scenarios that provide varied degrees of isolation between producers and consumers. Both the consumer and producer help to select the threading model used to pass events. The selection of a threading model is determined by which kind of producer or consumer class is used.

Figure 3.4 shows the different threading scenarios. In Figure 3.4, a T indicates a thread switch. In the scenario labeled 1, the event passes to the producer object and on to the consumer object in the producer class's thread. Queuing, dispatch, and event processing are all done on the producer's thread. This scenario provides no isolation between producers and consumers.

In the scenario labeled 2, the event passes to the producer object and on to the consumer object, at which time a thread switch occurs. This scenario isolates producers from event processing by the consumer but does not isolate producers from queuing and dispatch within the event manager.

In the scenario labeled 3, the event passes to the producer object and a thread switch occurs before the event is dispatched to the consumer object. This scenario also isolates producers from event processing by consumers but does not isolate consumers from queuing and dispatch within the event manager.

In the scenario labeled 4, the event passes to the producer object and a thread switch occurs. Another thread switch occurs at the consumer object. This scenario provides maximum isolation among all levels of the event system.

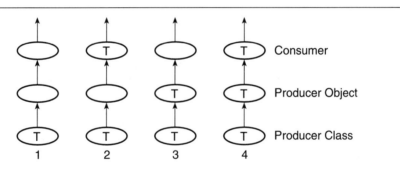

FIGURE 3.4   *Threading Scenarios*

3.8   Sample Device Driver Event

The following example describes, in general, the interrelationship between an event, the event system, and the various operating systems components involved in the process of locating and acknowledging a new device.

In this scenario, a PCI expansion board has been added to a network computer. For the board to function, a logical connection needs to be made between the board and the appropriate JavaOS device driver. As a result, the operating system first must recognize the new board, then pass the pertinent information to various OS system services. Once this process is complete, the new device can be matched with the appropriate device driver and function properly on the network.

The procedure to match a new device with its driver affects the JSD, the JSL, and the event system.

This scenario and the steps that follow assume that JavaOS has booted, and that the JSD, JSL, and other needed services are loaded. Furthermore, the JSD, during its initialization, registers with the event system as an exclusive producer of `EntryInsert` events. The JSL, during its initialization, subscribes to the event system as a consumer of `EntryInsert` events.

The following step numbers correspond to the steps found in Figure 3.5:

1. The device manager scans the JSD device tree looking for buses. For each bus discovered, the device manager calls the associated bus manager's `probe` method. In this example, the `probe` method activates the Peripheral Component Interface (PCI) expansion bus manager.

2. Once activated, the PCI expansion bus manager searches the PCI bus to determine if all connected devices are registered in the JSD Device tree. At this point, this specific PCI expansion board is not yet registered in the tree.

3. The PCI expansion bus manager recognizes that the new board is not registered in the JSD device tree. As a result, the bus manager inserts a JSD device entry (child) in the tree under the PCI bus entry (parent).

4. As acknowledgment of the insertion of the new device entry, the JSD generates an `EntryInsert` event. The event is passed to the event system.

5. The event system receives the JSD `EntryInsert` event and, through the event manager, identifies the JSL as a subscriber of `EntryInsert` events. Then the event system calls the JSL's `OSEventConsumer` handler to pass the event to the JSL.

6. The JSL receives the event and uses the device name in the event to search for a match between this event and all of the driver business cards. Once the JSL matches the device name with the correct driver business card, the PCI driver is assigned to the PCI device. At this point, the PCI expansion board is recognized as an active device on the network.

Figure 3.5 graphically depicts the process flow of the sample device driver event.

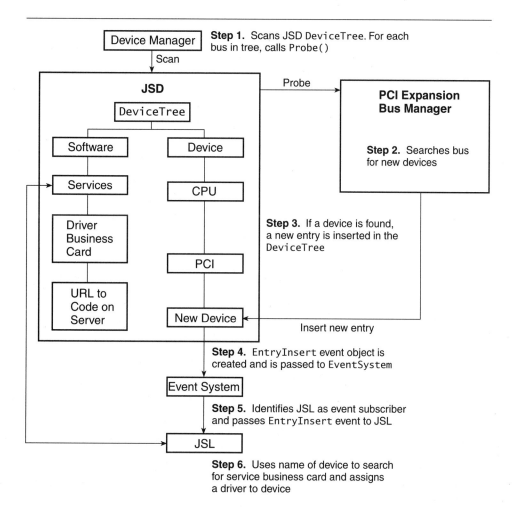

FIGURE 3.5 *Sample Device Driver Event Flow Chart*

3.9 Summary

An event is an object containing information that is exchanged between two other objects. The JavaOS event system provides a powerful, reliable, and secure mechanism by which objects can exchange events. Producers are objects that are the source of events. Consumers are objects that listen for events. The event manager is the code that sits in the middle, acting as the broker.

There are several advantages to using an event broker. Consumers can register in one place to receive events from all producers of events of that type. New producers of the event type can be added at any time, and existing consumers of the event type will automatically receive events from the new producer. Event queuing and dispatch code are centralized, and event delivery can be prioritized.

Chapter 4
The Service Loader

The JavaOS Service Loader (JSL) manages the loading and unloading of software components contained within a *bundle*. A bundle is a collection of Java components such as packages, applications, device drivers, resources, and data files defined by a *business card*. The business card is an object whose properties describe the bundle contents.

In the Java Runtime Enviroment, a class loader retrieves classes from sources external to the object heap. Once a class loads, the class loader resolves references to methods and variables in the class by loading other classes (that resolve the references) from the same external source.

Classes typically load from one or more file system directories defined by the CLASSPATH environment variable. When classes are needed to resolve references, the class loader finds classes in files. Class filenames are derived from a package and class name.

Package and class naming conventions give the class loader the ability to find classes. Unfortunately, device names don't adhere to the Java programming language class naming convention. The JSL provides a means of matching devices to their drivers. The JSL differs from a simple class loader in that it enables the identification, matching, and loading of services according to the capabilities that the service advertises in the JSD.

The JSL supports a variety of bundle container formats such as .JAR and .ZIP files, using a plug-in component called an *unbundler*.

The JSL minimizes the platform memory footprint by loading and activating services only as they are needed. The JSL is composed entirely of platform-independent code written in the Java programming language.

4.1   Services

A *service* is a bundle of code and data used to match devices with device drivers.
Service packages can be loaded on demand according to the capabilities they
advertise in the JSD Interface namespace.

JavaOS is composed of many services. Examples include device drivers, protocol stacks, file systems, and device managers. The only parts of JavaOS that are
not services are those components that always must be present and cannot be
replaced, such as the database and the JSL itself.

There are no restrictions on the type or number of classes that make up a service. The only requirement is that one or more classes must extend the `Service`
class and implement the `ServiceInstance` interface.

The `Service` class contains methods to start, stop, suspend, and resume a service.
A service can be started only once and stopped only once; in between, the service
can be suspended and resumed many times. Suspending a service disables its execution until it is resumed. The `Service` class also contains methods to retrieve the
business card for the service and the service's properties.

The `ServiceInstance` interface contains no methods. However, one class of
the service must implement this interface, and the implementing class must be identified in the service business card. The reason for this is that the JSL will look to the
identified class via introspection for a static method called `createInstance`.

```
public static ServiceInstance createInstance(Entry
businessCardEntry, String logicalName, Object parent, Entry
aliasEntry, Object cookie) throws ServiceException;
```

The JSL calls this method to create a new instance of the service.

The service can be partitioned into core and noncore classes. Core classes
instantiate on the client immediately when the service loads. Noncore classes are
downloaded to the client and instantiated only when actually used.

Services are loaded at different times, depending on the services' properties. The
service may be loaded when 1) the service is discovered, 2) a database entry associated with the service (usually a device) is discovered, or 3) the service is opened by a
client. Once loaded, services always execute on the client machine. A future version of
JavaOS might allow service execution to be partitioned between client and server.

4.2   Business Cards

The business-card class has properties that:

- Name the service
- Provide service vendor and versioning information

- Identify the service container file (.JAR or .ZIP)
- Provide configuration parameters for the service

The server-side JSD stores the business cards in the Config namespace. When a JavaOS client boots, all applicable service business cards download from the server into the client's JSD Software namespace. The JSL is a JSD event consumer. As business cards appear in the JSD, the JSD produces events that the JSL consumes, which causes the JSL to load and activate the associated services.

The business card contains the following information in the form of bean properties. Each property has a "get" and "set" method. When a service is installed in the JSD, each of these properties is converted to a JSD property associated with a business-card entry.

Title (String) A title for the service that displays to the user of the JavaOS Configuration Tool (JCT), which is described in the next section. The network administrator typically is the user of the JCT.

Icon (URL) A URL to a file containing an icon to represent the service. The JCT displays the icon when it manipulates the service business card. The JSL does not use the icon.

VendorName (URL) A URL of the vendor that created the service. The JCT also uses this field.

SourceCode (URL) An optional URL to the source code used to build the service. Debuggers use this field to support source-level debugging of services.

Major and Minor Version Numbers (Integers) Numbers used to discriminate between multiple versions of the same service.

Matching Name (String) A string used by the JSL to match a service with a device entry in the Device namespace. Some services load only when they are matched to their device. This chapter provides more details in Section 4.4 about so-called loading on matching.

Compatible Matching Names (Array of Strings) An array of strings providing alternative matching names to the JSL. The primary matching name is always used first.

Manager Name and Type (Strings) Name and type of the device manager for the driver. For example, the PCI drivers are associated with the PCI bus manager. See Chapter 6 for more details on device managers.

Loading Controls (Booleans) A set of three Booleans that control the loading characteristics of this service. See Section 4.4 for details.

Bundle Container (URL) A URL to a .ZIP or .JAR file containing the classes that implement the service.

Bundle Type (String) A string that names the container type for the service bundle. Currently, the JSL supports two types of containers: .ZIP and .JAR files. The bundle type also identifies the JSL unbundler for unpacking the bundle.

Bundle Initialization Class Name (String) The fully qualified name of the class implementing the `Service` interface (`java.system.service`). The previous section described the `Service` interface in more detail.

Bundle Package Name (String) The name of the service package. This name is used by the JSL to avoid class naming collisions. The classes and data files contained in each package must descend from a unique Java package prefix.

Bundle Class Path (URL) An alternative place to search for classes used by the service. The JSL uses this class path to find classes not in the bundle container.

Bundle Instance Info (String) A list of compound strings (comma-delineated lists), each string containing the information for loading, advertising, and referencing the service. Each string contains the logical instance name, the name of the class implementing the `ServiceInstance` interface, the name of the interface to be advertised, and an interface alias name.

Bundle Application Prefix Name (String) A unique prefix used to access data files within the container. The JSL uses this string to store a unique file prefix in the JDK system properties list. A service must retrieve this prefix in order to access data files in the service container.

4.3   The JavaOS Configuration Tool

The JCT is an applet written in the Java programming language that adds, deletes, and modifies information in the server-side JSD. The JCT adds users (people using JavaOS clients on the network) to the JSD and defines the services available to each user. The JCT also can associate users with groups of other users who share access to a set of services. The JCT can read business cards and extract and modify all the service properties listed in the previous section.

The JCT also is useful for configuring a particular JavaOS client, a group of clients, or a hardware platform (clients that are physically similar in some way). Using the JCT, the network administrator can specify which services are available on a particular client, group of clients, or platform, as well as login rules for each.

Once you specify all configuration parameters for a particular client machine, the JCT outputs a Master Configuration File (MCF) for the client. The MCF contains all information required to boot the client, such as the location of the system image and the services to load on booting. The existence of the MCF greatly simplifies the booting process because the client booter needs to read only a single file to determine all necessary information for getting the client up and running.

Figure 4.1 is a typical JCT screen shot. This sample panel lets a system administrator edit an existing user's configuration settings. The list of available settings and the currently configured settings are presented. To add a setting to a user's configuration, you select it from the available list on the right and click on the right arrow to add it to the configuration list on the left. If the setting itself needs to be configured, a popup panel lets you access the settings' own settings.

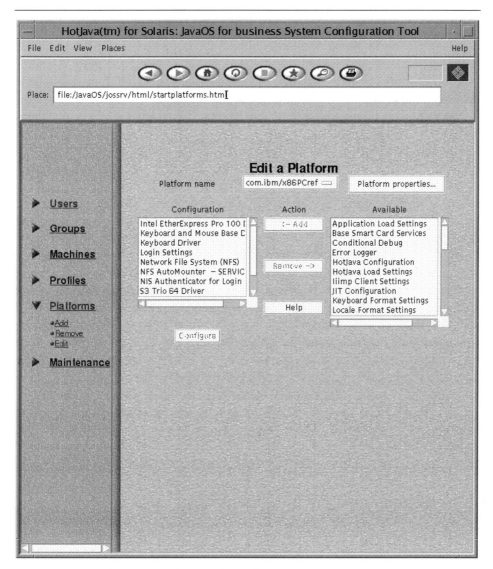

FIGURE 4.1 *A Typical JCT Screen Shot*

This panel lets the administrator assign a user to one or more groups of users by clicking on the "assign groups" button.

4.4   How the Service Loader Manages Services

The JSL loads, starts, stops, and unloads services. Several conditions can give rise to the loading of a service. For starters, a service can automatically load when JavaOS boots up.

The operating system's booter accomplishes loading on boot. The booter reads the MCF to obtain the list of services required to boot the machine. For each service listed in the MCF, the booter downloads the business card and code for the service into the client machine, loading the card and code into memory. When the booter starts the operating system, it gives the list of boot services to JavaOS and eventually the list is inserted into the software namespace of the JSD.

After booting, a service can load in other ways. First, a service can load automatically when the service is discovered, or, for example, when an entry for the service is inserted into the JSD. This is called *loading on discovery.* A service not advertised in the database at boot time can be subsequently advertised in the database of one or more clients using the JCT. Advertising the service generates an event, which leads to the JSL discovering the new service.

Another way to load a service after booting is upon discovery of a matching device entry in the database. This type of loading occurs only with device drivers. When JavaOS discovers a new piece of hardware and needs to load a matching driver, the JSL matches the device entry in the database with a business-card entry for the device driver and loads the driver. This is called *loading on matching.* The matching process involves scanning the Software namespace of the database for business cards of available services to locate one that identifies the device by name. Once the match is made, the driver is loaded and an entry is created in the Interface namespace for each interface the service (driver) implements. Each interface entry is called a *service advertisement* because it advertises to prospective clients of the driver the specific capabilities (interfaces) that the driver implements.

Finally, a service can be loaded on demand when the client actually requests its functions. This is called *loading on demand.* With loading on demand, the first attempt by a client to use a service causes the JSL to load and create an instance of the service. If another client wants to use the service, the service is not loaded again. A new instance of the service might be created, or else the second client might be connected to the existing instance. When the last client finishes with the service, the last service instance is unloaded and the garbage collector reclaims its resources.

Each time a service instance is created on the client, the JSL creates an entry identifying that instance and adds the entry to the Temp namespace of the database. This way, JavaOS can track each instance of every loaded service.

4.5 Downloading Services

The server stores the code and data for most services. However, services always execute on the client machine. In the current release of JavaOS, the server cannot remotely execute the services, and the execution of services cannot be partitioned between client and server. This might change in a future release of JavaOS.

The Config namespace in the server database stores business-card entries for all services available to a particular client. When the client is booted, all business cards for the client (listed in the MCF) are downloaded from the server database to the client database, where they are stored in the Software namespace. The loading parameter in the business card determines when the service code downloads. For loading on boot or loading on discovery, the code for the service will download immediately from the server when the business card is discovered. For loading on matching, the service code downloads when the service matches with a device or other database entry. For loading on demand, the service code downloads only when a client actually uses the service.

The server stores service classes together in a container file, which usually is a .ZIP or .JAR file. Other service classes can be stored outside the container (the service business card is a good example). There is no requirement that all code classes for the service be stored inside the container.

As business cards download from the server for insertion into the Software namespace, matching and advertisement occurs, as explained in the previous section. An event is generated each time a service advertisement is inserted in the Interface namespace. Clients can be alerted to the availability of particular types of services by subscribing to events from particular branches of the Interface namespace.

For example, a client interested in obtaining the services of a fax driver could subscribe to events from the Fax subtree of the Interface namespace. When a service advertisement for a fax driver is inserted into the Fax subtree, an event is sent to the client and the client can respond by opening the driver.

4.6 Connecting Clients and Services

Each JavaOS client is assigned a subtree of the server database. This subtree holds all configuration information for the client, including which services are available to the client both during and after booting. Business cards identify services. When the client boots, all business cards for the client download from the server subtree to the client's Software namespace. The client can access only those services for which a business-card entry exists in its Software namespace.

The JSL connects clients with services that meet their interface requirements. It is up to the client to initiate and drive the connection process. A client constructs a service connection object and calls the methods of this object to instruct the JSL to find a service implementing a particular interface. For example, clients of the Fax interface connect with services that implement the Fax interface. If more than one service implements the desired interface, the client, with the assistance of the JSL, decides which service to use. Once the client selects a service, it calls the service methods through the service connection object. Services themselves can be clients of other services and, in fact, this is often the case. For example, a file system service can call the methods of a disk drive service.

The following code fragment shows how a client can request an enumeration of services compatible with a named interface. Given the enumeration, the client then can select which service to open.

The findAdvertisements method is part of the ServiceLoader class. It returns the enumeration of service advertisements for a given interface name.

```
public static Enumeration findAdvertisements(String
advertisedInterface) throws ServiceException

ServiceAdvertisement a;
String interfaceName = "/javaos/javax/system/jdi/fax/";
String serviceName = "Marketing Group Fax";
Enumeration faxes;

faxes = ServiceLoader.findAdvertisements(interfaceName);
while(faxes.hasMoreElements()) {
    a = (ServiceAdvertisement)faxes.nextElement();
    if (a.getLogicalName() = serviceName)
        break;
}
```

To retrieve a service connection object for the desired service, the service advertisement is passed to the findService method. For example, to retrieve an instance of a particular fax driver:

```
public static ServiceConnection findService(ServiceAdvertisement
serviceAdvertisement) throws ServiceException

ServiceConnection s;
s= ServiceLoader.findService(a);
```

In this last example, the variable *a* represents the service advertisement that the client indentified in the preceding example as most suitable to its requirements.

Once the service connection object is retrieved, the client connects to the service by calling the connect method.

```
s.connect(parentServiceInstance);
```

The parentServiceInstance parameter allows a parent-child service relationship to be formed that is useful for services, such as device drivers, that cooperate in a hierachical fashion with other services.

Calling `connect` loads (if necessary) and instantiates the service classes. When the JSL loads a service class, it passes the service's business card to the service, so that the device has access to its own properties. To disconnect from the service, call *disconnect*.

```
s.disconnect();
```

When the last client of the service disconnects, the service is unloaded.

4.7 Service Loader Architecture

Figure 4.2 shows the architecture of the service loader. In this figure, a client of some service (recall that the client itself can be a service) instantiates a service connection class object. The client identifies the type of service it is interested in connecting to, typically by specifying an applicable interface. The service connection class invokes the JSL to provide a list of matching services. The JSL fulfills this request by scanning the Interface namespace of the database for matching service advertisements. A list of matching services is returned to the client. The client selects which service to use, then requests to open the service. If the service is already loaded, the service connection object merely returns an instance of the service to the client. Otherwise, the service connection object passes the open

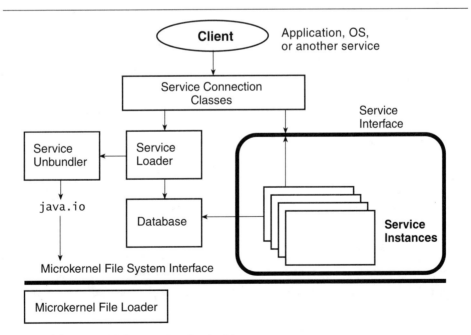

FIGURE 4.2 *JavaOS Service Loader Architecture*

request along to the JSL, which then initiates the downloading of the service container file. Once downloaded, the container file is passed to an unbundler that extracts the service class files. The JSL instantiates the service, and the service connection object returns the service instance to the client.

An *unbundler* exists for every bundle type. The unbundler can unpack .ZIP, .JAR, or other container files to extract the service classes. The unbundler uses `java.io` file services that, in turn, use the low-level file system services of the microkernel to download the service container file from the host server. The JSL reads the name of the container file for the service classes from the service's business card. It passes this file name to the unbundler. Once the classes have been unbundled, the JSL instantiates the service classes. Instantiation of a service class causes the JSL to create a tracking entry for the service object in the JSD Temp namespace.

The JSL uses the JSD to track instances of services. A private tracking entry is created in the JSD's Temp namespace for this purpose. Figure 4.3 illustrates how the JSL uses the JSD to track and refer to service instances.

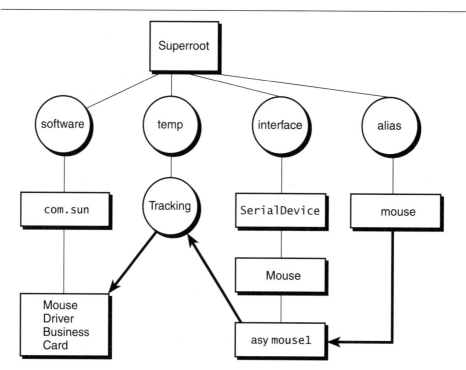

FIGURE 4.3   *Business Card Tracking Entries Cross-Reference Interfaces
           and Services*

4.8 Summary

JSL manages the loading and unloading of software components contained within a *bundle*.

Package and class naming conventions give the class loader the ability to find classes. The JSL provides a means of matching devices to their drivers. It differs from a simple class loader in that it enables identification, matching, and loading according to the capabilities that a service advertises in the JSD.

Chapter 5
Standard Device Support

Most network computers running JavaOS software must support a standard set of devices expected by most software written in the Java programming language: the network adaptor, video adaptor, mouse, and keyboard. Supporting standard devices is more complicated than supporting embedded platform devices such as interrupt controllers and serial port controllers. Standard I/O devices, in theory, can be swapped out by the end user and replaced with devices from different manufacturers. This chapter explains how JavaOS supports these standard devices while maintaining the promise of platform neutrality.

5.1 Networking

Three components provide JavaOS networking support:

- A network device driver
- An implementation of `java.net`
- A protocol stack for connecting the `java.net` classes with the network driver

The network device driver is responsible for reading and writing data packets to and from the network adaptor. The `java.net` implementation classes provide standard JDK API support for networking, and the protocol stack implements the communication protocols of the attached network. All three components are platform-independent, but the driver is device- and bus-dependent.

5.1.1   Networking Architecture

Figure 5.1 shows the JavaOS networking architecture. The discussion of the architecture is framed in terms of data received from the network. With minor modifications, these details apply equally to data transmitted to the network.

The JavaOS Platform Interface (JPI) is at the lowest level of the networking system. The JPI provides memory and interrupt functions to the network driver, which sits directly above it. When the network adapter receives a data packet from the network, direct memory access (DMA) places the packet in the Java heap. An interrupt is dispatched to the network device driver via the JPI and a thread within the driver is activated to service the DMA completion interrupt. The data packet then is transformed into a packet object and begins its journey up the protocol stack. Figure 5.2 captures the journey of a received packet up through layers of the system.

As shown in Figure 5.2, the adaptor generates an interrupt that is dispatched to the driver via the JPI interrupt classes. The driver then reads the data packet from memory using the JPI memory classes. The memory and interrupt functionality is implemented natively by the microkernel. The data packet is not copied. Rather, it is read by the network adaptor driver by creating an object with a reference to the data packet memory location. This object is called the packet object. The protocol stack uses the packet object to reference and analyze the data packet without performing a memory copy.

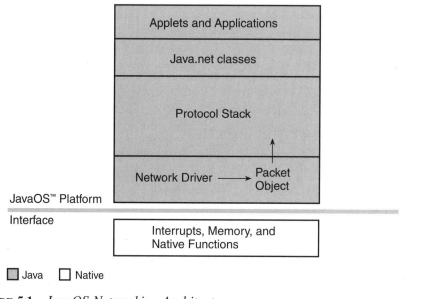

FIGURE 5.1 *JavaOS Networking Architecture*

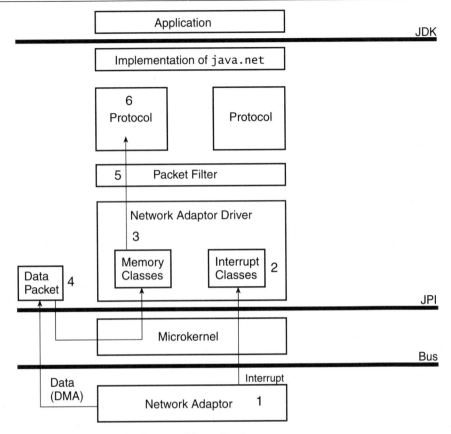

FIGURE 5.2 *Journey of a Received Data Packet*

The driver passes the packet object to a layer called the *packet filter*, which technically is not part of the protocol stack. Because the protocol stack is written entirely in the Java programming language, the stack can be loaded on demand according to the protocols that the network uses. The packet filter is responsible for analyzing the packet header for routing to the appropriate protocol layer. Once the packet reaches the proper protocol stack, the packet is analyzed and routed to the proper applet or application.

5.1.2 Platform-Independent Networking

The network driver is a device driver, written completely in the Java programming language, that calls a single native method to accelerate the computation of check-sum values. This native method is hardware-independent—it can be called by any driver for any particular device that needs to compute checksums. Thus, if the native method is present on all platforms, the network driver is platform-independent, even though it calls a native method. This is important because it demonstrates that a device driver that calls a native method can be platform-independent, so long as the native method is implemented on all platforms on which the driver runs. The network adaptor can be upgraded or replaced dynamically, reducing maintenance and upgrade costs.

It is not always possible to write drivers without employing hardware-specific native acceleration routines. This is particularly true of devices such as video adaptors that have very high performance requirements. On the other hand, as bytecode compilation technologies improve, the necessity for native acceleration routines diminish.

Additionally, a well-designed driver can include optimizations to decrease the necessity for native methods. The networking system, for example, avoids repeated memory copies by retaining the data packet in the DMA memory location to which it was originally copied by the network adaptor. The `packet` object that is passed to the protocol stack contains only a reference to the actual data packet.

The network driver uses the JPI to achieve platform independence so that the driver is not dependent on the byte ordering, interrupt scheme, or memory model of the underlying hardware. A driver can be written for a particular network adaptor and bus combination without having to port the code to different platforms. For example, a single Ethernet driver could run on platforms without porting, using, for example, one of the following:

- SPARC CPU and a Peripheral Component Interconnect (PCI) bus
- x86 CPU and a PCI bus
- PowerPC CPU equipped with a PCI bus

5.2   Video

The JavaOS video system connects applet and application clients of the `java.awt` classes to the video hardware. The video system consists of the following components written in the Java programming language:

- Video device driver
- Windowing and graphics classes
- Classes that implement `java.awt`

And the following native software component:

- Native video acceleration methods

In contrast to the networking system, the classes of the video system often require a substantial body of native code to achieve desirable performance levels.

5.2.1   Video Operation

There are two stages to video system operation: initialization and I/O. Initialization involves:

- Configuring the video adaptor to operate in a particular video mode
- Synchronizing the video adaptor with the associated monitor to ensure compatible refresh rates and video modes
- Loading the video adaptor palette with the system colors to map pixel values into actual RGB colors for display

Video I/O is the process of writing pixels to the display device frame buffer. Video I/O operations include rendering primitive graphics operations (such as drawing lines, filling regions with a solid color, and drawing arcs) to the display and clipping the rendered graphics primitives to fit in the drawing area of the client window.

Figure 5.3 illustrates the interaction of the video system, the video display adaptor, and the display during the initialization and I/O stages of operation.

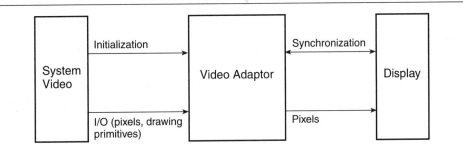

FIGURE 5.3   *Video Initialization and I/O*

5.2.2   Video Architecture

The JavaOS video architecture supports video initialization and I/O with no performance compromise. To achieve good performance, the video driver is a hybrid of Java software and native acceleration methods. The native methods are used for clipping, building device-specific pixels, and rendering graphics primitives. Figure 5.4 shows a detailed diagram of the components of the video system.

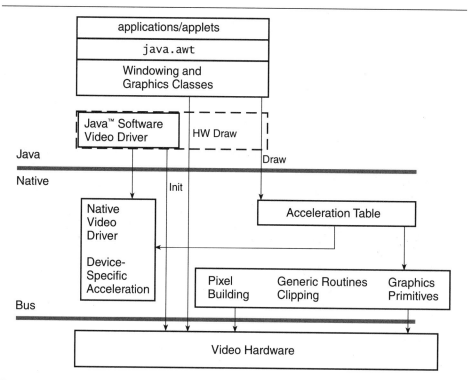

FIGURE 5.4 *JavaOS Video System*

For performance reasons the video system relies heavily on native methods. Not all video adaptors will require native method support, but most will. If the video adaptor uses hardware acceleration for rendering graphics primitives, then a one-hundred percent Java software video system is feasible because the rendering occurs in hardware, not software. More and more video adaptors are incorporating hardware acceleration. It might be only a matter of time before Java software, loadable-on-demand video drivers are commonplace.

The native acceleration methods divide into initialization methods and I/O methods. The initialization methods are invoked once, as the driver is loaded, to perform the one-time initializations: setting the video mode, synchronizing the adaptor and monitor, and configuring the color palette. Once initialization is complete, the I/O methods are used to write pixels to the display. The initialization methods install device-specific acceleration methods for I/O and then get out of the way.

The I/O methods are divided into generic and device-specific categories. Generic methods are available on all JavaOS platforms that are hardware-independent and provide a least-common-denominator approach to video acceleration, using device-independent C algorithms. Hardware-dependent acceleration methods take advantage of hardware optimizations. Other native methods perform clipping, and still others convert device-independent RGB values into device-specific pixel values of 8, 16, or 32 bits.

Filling a rectangular region of the display with a solid color is an example of a graphics primitive that can be accelerated. This operation is invoked frequently by the windowing classes to draw window backgrounds, title bars, and large areas with a single solid color. Another operation highly suited to acceleration is the rectangular blit copy, which fills a rectangular area of the display with pixel values from another rectangular area of the display. Other candidates for acceleration are vector line drawing primitives, text display operations, and system memory-to-display blits. This last operation is useful for displaying images from Web pages.

Device-specific native acceleration methods are installed by replacing the generic method entry points in the native acceleration table with device-specific entry points. When the windowing and graphics classes invoke the entry points in the table, they are vectored to the device-specific methods instead of to the generic ones. Because the device-specific entry points transparently replace the generic entry points, the device-specific methods must implement the same interface contract as do the generic methods. Ironically, the device-specific methods might in turn invoke the generic methods if, once the parameters to the method are an-lyzed, the device-specific methods determine that the particular video operation cannot take advantage of device-specific optimizations.

For video devices that support hardware acceleration, native code might be unnecessary. With these devices, the windowing and graphics classes can call through an abstract class that implements the device-specific optimizations through calls to the JPI. Concrete instances of this class can be manufactured and provided to the graphics and windowing classes by the video driver.

5.2.3 Alternative Video Designs

The acceleration table is one way for the video subsystem to invoke device-specific code transparently. Another way is through conditional compilation of the JavaOS native code base. For example, consider the following native entry point, visible to the windowing and graphics classes, called DrawPixel.

```
void DrawPixel (RGB rgb, Point pt)
```

The purpose of this native method is to convert a device-independent RGB value into a device-specific pixel of a depth of 8, 16, or 32 bits, and then to draw that pixel at the specified coordinate on the display. The source code for this native method can include code for performing all four conversions—RGB to 8 bit, RGB to 16 bit, and so on. Conditional compilation statements are used to select the implementation for a particular device. The advantage of this approach is speed—no `if` statements are required in a native routine where performance is crucial. The disadvantage of this approach is that it ties the JavaOS native code base to a particular video device (or family of devices in the case of pixel conversion).

An alternative approach that maintains the device neutrality of the JavaOS native code base is to include separate `DrawPixel` methods for each pixel depth within the JavaOS native base. The single generic method then is replaced by four methods: `DrawPixel8`, `DrawPixel16`, `DrawPixel24`, and `DrawPixel32`. The windowing and graphics classes invoke the proper version of `DrawPixelX` by calling through an abstract class that encapsulates the device-specific native call. The video driver manufactures and provides to the graphics and windowing classes concrete instances of this class. Another alternative is that the implementation of `DrawPixel` simply includes a switch statement to select the proper pixel depth. Both techniques maintain the device neutrality of the JavaOS native code base but have the disadvantage of being slower: the first because of the indirection incurred in the process of calling through a concrete implementation of an abstract class, the second because of the switch statement.

In general, if device-specific methods are installed to accelerate graphics primitives, then the device neutrality of the JavaOS native code base has already been compromised, and there is no reason not to conditionally compile for the correct pixel depth. It also might be desirable to remove from the native code base any generic acceleration methods not used by a particular video device. This keeps the native code base uncluttered by unused code

The video system is an example of device support implemented with performance as the overarching consideration, to the detriment of platform independence. Video drivers with hardware-dependent native components cannot be considered platform-independent, although they can encapsulate the hardware-dependence into a relatively small body of native code and distill out the platform-independent portions into Java code. Such hybrid JavaOS drivers usually perform better than Java software drivers. However, because of their hardware-specific components, hybrid drivers are more difficult to port, upgrade, and maintain, and they are not loadable on demand by the JavaOS Service Loader.

In general, video driver writers should take advantage of hardware-specific optimizations. However, the advantages in portability, maintainability, and dynamic installation sometimes can outweigh the performance advantage that is gained by incorporating hardware-specific code into the driver.

5.3   Mouse Support

JavaOS supports various types of peripheral mice, including a PC-style serial mouse. Because it exemplifies the use of layered drivers in JavaOS, the serial mouse is described here. A layered driver model is one in which device drivers are organized hierarchically: upper-level drivers call upon the services of lower-level drivers to control a device attached to an expansion bus or communication port.

To read input and motion coordinates from the mouse, a serial mouse driver must call upon the device driver for the serial port. Thus, the serial mouse driver is layered upon the serial port driver. Figure 5.5 illustrates this relationship.

Communicating with a serial port driver, rather than directly with the port controller driver, enables the serial mouse driver to operate independently of the actual port-controller chip. Some serial ports will use the more-or-less standard UART16550 controller chip; others might use a more advanced port controller (perhaps one with a larger FIFO, small FIFO size being one of the main criticisms of the UART16550). The serial port driver in turn communicates directly with the port-controller driver, which is specific to the port-controller chip.

Creating a layered driver architecture in Java software is easy. You could implement the serial mouse architecture in the following way:

```
class SerialMouseDriver
abstract class SerialPortDriver
class UART16550Driver extends SerialPortDriver
```

Then, to use the services of the serial port, the mouse driver simply instantiates the UART16550 driver class and calls the generic (controller-independent) methods of `SerialPortDriver`. However, by explicitly instantiating the port-controller driver, the mouse driver becomes dependent upon the port controller, a situation to be avoided using the layered architecture. The solution to this dilemma is to create a driver `factory`, which instantiates and returns the serial port driver to the mouse driver:

```
public class CommPortIdentifier
public SerialPortDriver open (String commPort)
```

The `Factory` class is called `CommPortIdentifier`. It has an `open` method that takes a string containing the logical port name (COM1, COM2, and so on) and returns the corresponding serial port driver. The actual concrete class returned

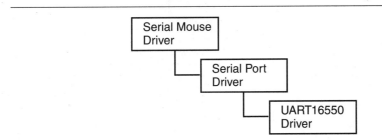

FIGURE 5.5 *Layered Driver Architecture for a Serial Mouse Device*

could be an extension of SerialPortDriver, such as the UART16550Driver port-controller driver. In other words, the concrete return class is specific to the port controller for the logical port specified in the open call. Once the mouse driver has the serial driver object, it can perform serial I/O through the serial driver's methods without ever knowing which port controller the serial port is using.

The CommPortIdentifier Factory class could be a static class (in which case no instantiation of the Factory class is required by the mouse driver), or it could be a nonstatic class that the mouse driver must instantiate. In either case, the mouse driver must call the open method to retrieve a concrete serial driver class.

We can extend this factory concept one step higher, so that the object returned by the open method represents *any* communication port, not just serial ports:

```
public class CommPortIdentifier
public CommPortDriver open (String commPort)
abstract class SerialPortDriver extends CommPortDriver
```

When the serial mouse driver retrieves the concrete driver class from CommPortIdentifier, it must cast the returned class to a SerialPortDriver. Communicating with serial ports is different from communicating with other types of ports (such as parallel ports) because there are different events to trap, different status indicators, and so on. Think of the serial communication port to which the mouse is attached as a bus. Remember from earlier chapters that drivers are device- and bus-specific. The serial mouse driver is not also a parallel mouse driver and cannot be abstracted to that level. Figure 5.6 illustrates the resulting hierarchy.

The mouse driver includes code similar to the following, for connecting to the mouse port in a platform-independent manner:

```
public SerialMouseDriver {

SerialPortDriver cp = (SerialPortDriver)
CommPortIdentifier.open("COM1");
```

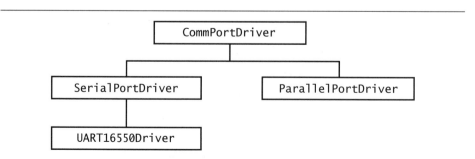

FIGURE 5.6 *Communication Port Driver Hierarchy*

```
if (dataAvailable)
cp.read(bytes[]);

}
```

Of course, this is a simplification of what the serial mouse driver actually does. The driver, for instance, probably would create a separate I/O thread to read from the mouse device and would respond to serial port events indicating the availability of new data. Also, following standard JDK convention, the actual I/O read method could be encapsulated into an `InputStream` object.

The port driver might require a native component for servicing interrupts from the serial port controller. Some serial port controllers, especially the UART16550, have very small input FIFOs and the risk of data overruns is great unless the FIFOs can be serviced with low interrupt latency.

5.4 Keyboard Support

The keyboard device support in JavaOS exemplifies how the Java programming language lends itself to system-level programming. A substantial amount of the operating system code is dedicated to receiving data from shared devices and, at higher levels of the system, to routing the data to multiple software components. The Java programming language's object-oriented design and support for threading enable such system coding to be implemented in an intuitively straightforward manner. Figure 5.7 shows the general architecture of the input data routing system in JavaOS.

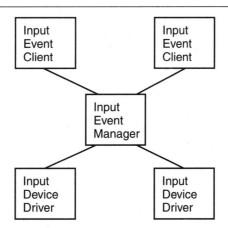

FIGURE 5.7 *General Input Data Routing Architecture*

At the lowest level of the system are multiple-input device drivers that respond to interrupts (or poll) data input devices, such as the keyboard and mouse drivers. An input device that uses interrupts will interrupt when data is available. The device driver receives the interrupt and responds by reading the available data from the device. In the case of a keyboard device, the event that precipitates these activities is the pressing of a key by the user.

Reading the data is only the beginning of the process. Next, the data must be transformed into a format that is understandable by higher layers of the system. In the case of a mouse, a relative x,y offset value pair must be translated into absolute screen coordinates and logical window coordinates. In the case of a keyboard, the raw scancode generated by the keystroke must be translated into a virtual keycode that is independent of the particular keyboard model or language. This translation is accomplished using a `Key Table` class for the installed keyboard. Figure 5.8 shows how the keyboard driver uses the `Key Table` class to "virtualize" the keystroke.

How does the keyboard driver know which key table class to pass the raw scancode to? With only a single key table in the system, the driver simply passes the scancode to the only available key table. Another possibility is that the driver itself might contain the key table. Both of these options have limitations. When there is only one key table, the system will not support more than one type of keyboard. When the driver itself contains the key table, different keyboard drivers are unable to take advantage of the ability to use the same key table, even when they support the same or similar keyboard models.

One solution that works well is to create a generic translation class to map scancodes to virtual keycodes. This translation class can use a `Factory` class to create a key table object corresponding to the particular model of installed keyboard. The `Translation` class then simply passes the scancode to the manufactured `Key Table` class to perform the translation. Figure 5.9 illustrates this approach.

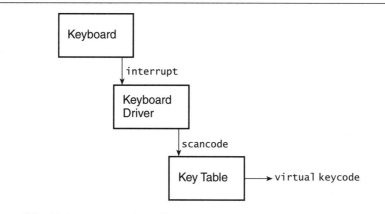

FIGURE 5.8 *Using a* Key Table *Class*

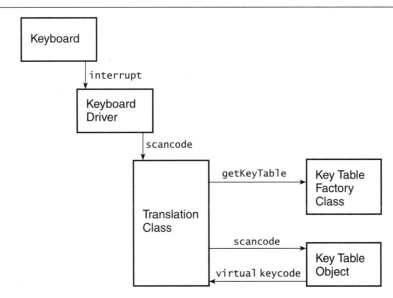

FIGURE 5.9   *Using a* Key Table Factory *Class*

In simplified Java software, the implementation looks like this:

```
class keyboard_driver {
    public void keyboard_driver () {
        //instantiate key translation class
        KeyTranslationClass trans_class = System.getKBDTransClass();
    }
    void interrupt_handler() {
        scancode = memory.read(KBD_INP);
        trans_class.input(scancode);

    }
}
class KeyTranslationClass {
InputEventManager iem;

public void KeyTranslationClass {
    //system manufactures key table
    KeyTable kt = System.getKeyTable();
}

public void input (int scancode) {
    //map scancode to virtual key
    VirtualKey vk = kt.map (scancode);
    //pass virtual key to input event
    manager for distribution
    //to input event clients
    iem.pressKey (vk);
}
```

```
public void registerInputEventManager
(InputEventManager inevmg) {
    iem = inevmg;
    }
}
```

Notice that a class called System is used as a factory for both the Key Translation class and the Key Table class. Once the keystroke is in a virtual (hardware-independent) format, the next step is to make the keystroke available to all system software components that monitor keyboard inputs. This is accomplished by calling the input event manager class (see Figure 5.7). This class converts the keystroke into an event object and broadcasts the event object to all input event clients.

The event input manager must perform a context switch to remove the keystroke data from the interrupt thread of the keyboard device driver. A low-latency context switch is accomplished by placing the keystroke event into a FIFO that is monitored by a separate thread within the input event manager (called the dispatch thread). The dispatch thread dispatches the event to registered input event clients. Figure 5.10 shows this thread switch within the input event manager.

In Java software, the context switch and event dispatch code look something like this:

```
class InputEventManager {
    private static EventFIFO fifo;

    public void pressKey (VirtualKey vk) {
        Event ev = new Event((Object) vk);
        fifo.add (ev);
    }
```

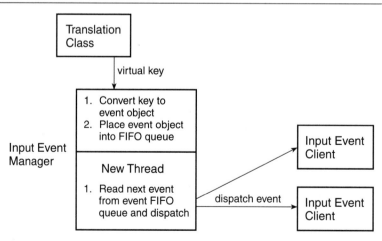

FIGURE 5.10　*Dispatching Keyboard Events*

```
    public void run () {

    while (TRUE) {
        Event ev = fifo.get();
        //dispatch to registered input clients
        for(i=0; inumInputClients;i++)
        inputclients[i].inputEventHandler(eu)
    }
  }
}
```

Notice that the EventFIFO is static: all instances of the input event manager share the same FIFO. This approach simplifies system design and ensures that all keyboard events are processed in the order received. The example uses a crude iterative dispatch loop. In reality, the input event manager would invoke the services of the JavaOS Event System, which in turn uses a more sophisticated dispatch mechanism.

5.5 Summary

JavaOS provides support for the standard set of devices expected by most Java software: the network adaptor, video adaptor, mouse, and keyboard. The support for these devices consists of a collection of I/O host classes and a set of device drivers. The classes and drivers are written largely in the Java programming language, reducing the dependency on native code typically found in a host OS.

Chapter 6
Device Drivers

Most operating systems provide a mechanism for moving data to and from the outside world. This mechanism usually involves device drivers, which are software components for controlling and performing I/O with a device. Most operating systems also set forth design rules for writing drivers so that they may interact with the system in a standard way. Figure 6.1 shows the place drivers occupy in JavaOS.

JavaOS device drivers are written in the Java programming language and, therefore, are CPU-independent. Drivers also are platform-independent because they access memory and interrupts using objects from the JavaOS Platform Interface (JPI). A *platform* is defined to be one or more CPUs, the physical memory available to those CPUs, and any permanently attached devices or buses. Although platform-independent, JavaOS device drivers are specific to a particular device and bus combination.[1]

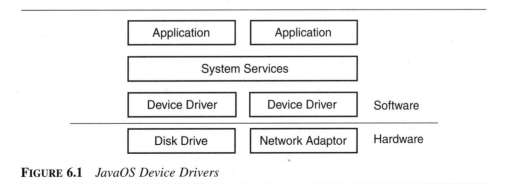

FIGURE 6.1 *JavaOS Device Drivers*

---

1. Although it is possible to design an operating system that enables the creation of bus-independent device drivers, the overhead of doing so has typically outweighed the benefits.

6.1   Connecting Devices

Devices connect to a platform in several ways. One way is directly to the CPU address or I/O bus. Devices connected in this manner are directly addressable by the CPU and are called *platform devices*. A second way to connect devices is using an *expansion bus*. An expansion bus expands the number of devices that may be addressed directly by the CPU by mapping device memory ranges to the CPU's physical address space. Expansion buses are controlled by an expansion bus chip set that connects the expansion bus to the CPU's address bus and/or internal I/O bus. Examples of expansion buses are Peripheral Component Interconnect (PCI) and Industry Standard Architecture (ISA).

A third way to connect devices to the platform is using an *external I/O bus,* which connects by way of an external I/O bus controller. This controller may connect directly to the CPU address bus or to an expansion bus. The Small Computer System Interface (SCSI) bus is a common example of an external I/O bus. A SCSI controller chip may be mounted directly on the platform motherboard, acting as a direct interface between the CPU address bus and the external SCSI I/O bus. Alternatively, a SCSI controller adaptor card may be installed in an expansion bus slot on the platform. The SCSI bus controller connects to the expansion bus controller by way of the expansion bus, and the expansion bus controller connects to the CPU address bus. Figure 6.2 illustrates the various ways of connecting devices to the platform.

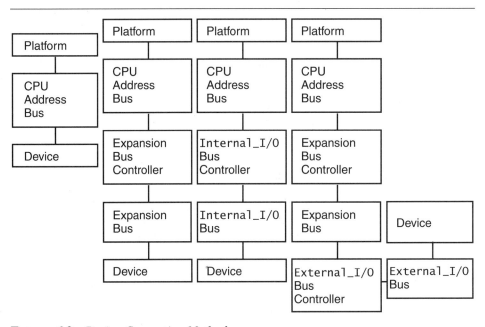

FIGURE 6.2 *Device Connection Methods*

Another type of device is worth mentioning at this point. A *virtual device* is the emulation of the behavior of a hardware device in software. A virtual device is not physically connected to the platform at all; its existence is purely a software construction. However, a virtual device is treated as though it connected directly to the CPU address bus like a platform device would.

Later in this chapter we will see the software components used to manage devices connected in these different ways.

6.2   Life Cycle of a Device Driver

A driver is loaded either separately or as part of the JavaOS boot image. A driver that is included in the boot image is, of course, loaded at boot time. It is called a *static* driver. Static drivers usually are fast and indispensable, but otherwise they are uninteresting. They cannot be unloaded without shutting down the system; they cannot be swapped out without replacing the kernel. *Dynamic* drivers are much more interesting. Dynamic drivers can be loaded and unloaded on demand, dynamically matched with devices, replaced and upgraded—all while the OS is running. The following discussion pertains only to dynamic drivers.

Device drivers begin their life cycle by being discovered. Discovery of devices takes place during booting, and possibly later in the case of removable devices such as PCMCIA devices. At boot time, devices are discovered when the booter provides the JavaOS Runtime Environment with a device tree describing the available devices and how they are connected to the platform. An entry for the device is created within the JSD and is named. Naming allows the device to be referenced using a friendly name or alias. The device is now part of the system and is off line, waiting to be matched with a driver.

Next, a driver is located for the device (through a process described later). The device is now on line and ready for use. However, the driver will not be loaded until a software client actually requests to perform I/O with the device. This is called opening the device. Once a device is open for I/O, it changes status from idle to busy and back again as I/O requests are made. Finally, when the client is done with the device the driver is closed.

6.3   Architecture of JavaOS Drivers

JavaOS uses a shallow driver architecture. A shallow architecture avoids excessive architectural levels while at the same time simplifying the task of writing drivers by centralizing common functions. In many cases, the architecture is only two or three levels deep, with clients invoking driver methods through only one or two intervening levels. In rare cases, a client may need to call through three or more levels to reach the methods in a device driver.

The JavaOS device driver architecture consists of two levels. The lowest level is the *device driver* itself. A device driver controls and exchanges data with the device and, therefore, is specific to the device. Above the driver is a more abstract, device-independent level of functionality called the *device manager.*

The device manager contains functions that are common across a category of devices. For example, all audio devices share certain common characteristics that are implemented in JavaOS by a single audio device manager. Implementation details specific to particular audio devices are implemented by multiple audio device drivers (assuming there are multiple audio devices connected to the platform).

The basic two-level driver architecture is illustrated in Figure 6.3 (the client is not part of the architecture per se). The device manager not only acts as a common entry point to drivers within a device category, it also provides the drivers below it with functionality common to the device category. This centralizes the common functions in one location and makes the job of writing drivers easier. Sometimes, a device is so unique that it does not belong to any category for which common functions exist. In this case, the device driver and device manager merge and clients interact directly with the driver. The driver must implement the standard device manager client interface in this case.

For example, the SCSI bus functionality is divided between a single SCSI bus manager and multiple SCSI bus drivers. Each driver is matched to a particular SCSI chip set implementation, while the SCSI bus manager implements chip-set-independent functionality and exports it to the drivers. For PCI buses, no such division of labor is possible; the PCI specification is specific enough that all PCI bus drivers look basically the same. It wouldn't make sense to have a PCI bus manager separate from the driver, because little or no implementation-specific code would end up in the driver—the PCI bus manager would be the whole thing.

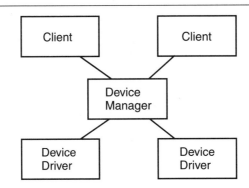

FIGURE 6.3   *Two-level Driver Architecture*

A special type of device driver called a *bus driver* is associated with a bus controller. There are two general types of bus drivers: *expansion bus drivers* and *drivers for external I/O buses*. From this point on, a nonbus device driver is referred to as simply a device driver.

From a device driver's point of view, the main purpose of an expansion bus driver is to act as a source of memory and interrupt objects for devices on the bus. The expansion bus driver provides the device driver with objects representing the memory regions for addressing the device and the interrupts used by the device. The expansion bus driver does not get involved in control or data exchange between the device driver and the device. Instead, the device driver interacts with the device through the JPI memory and interrupt objects manufactured for it by the expansion bus driver.

Bus drivers for external I/O buses take a more active role in device control, serving as a gateway for control and data exchange between device drivers and devices connected to the external I/O bus.

Bus drivers are simply a special form of device drivers. Therefore, the architecture for bus drivers is divided into the same two basic layers as the architecture for device drivers. At the lower level are the drivers themselves, each of which controls a specific implementation of a bus-control chip set. For each category of bus, a single bus manager exists with generic functionality common across the bus category. This is true for both expansion and external I/O buses. For example, a SCSI bus is managed using two basic components: a SCSI-controller chip set driver for a particular controller implementation, and a SCSI bus manager containing functionality common to all SCSI controllers.

Figure 6.4 shows drivers and managers for both devices and buses interacting within a typical I/O stack.

The figure shows the I/O stack between an application and a SCSI CD ROM device. The application communicates with the block read/write methods of a `Partition Manager` object. This object is like a device manager for block I/O devices—it performs generic format/control operations for block I/O devices and then passes I/O requests along to specific driver implementations.

The `Partition Manager` can communicate I/O requests to any block device driver that implements the `Partition` interface, in this case, the SCSI CD ROM driver. The SCSI CD ROM driver implements the `Partition` interface and performs device-specific formatting and control. To move the data over the SCSI bus, the SCSI CD ROM driver invokes the I/O methods of a SCSI bus manager, which in turn invokes a chip-set-specific implementation object to communicate with the bus hardware. Finally, the chip set driver uses the JPI to access device memory and interrupts.

Device drivers format data for devices and control devices. Bus drivers, which are simply device drivers for buses, format data for buses and control buses. As straightforward as this sounds, sometimes it is easier to think of buses not as

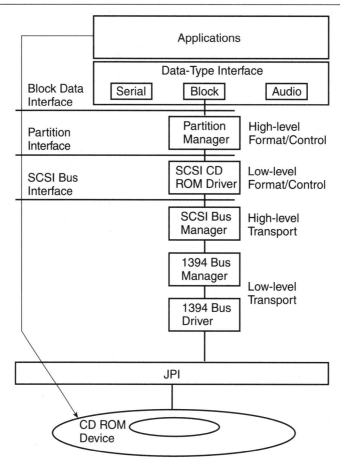

FIGURE 6.4 *Typical I/O Stack*

devices but as mechanisms for transporting data between devices. Buses become a transport mechanism for data. The figure reflects this perspective, labeling the SCSI bus manager as providing high-level transport services to the device driver and the SCSI chip-set driver as providing low-level transport services to the SCSI bus driver.

The left side of the figure shows the public I/O interfaces associated with each object in the I/O stack. The right side shows the objects at each level of the stack. Beginning at the application, data flows down the stacks until it reaches the SCSI CD ROM device itself.

The next figure (Figure 6.5) is identical to the preceding one, except that now the SCSI adapter is connected to the platform through a PCI expansion bus. The stack now includes an additional component in the form of a PCI Manager/Driver

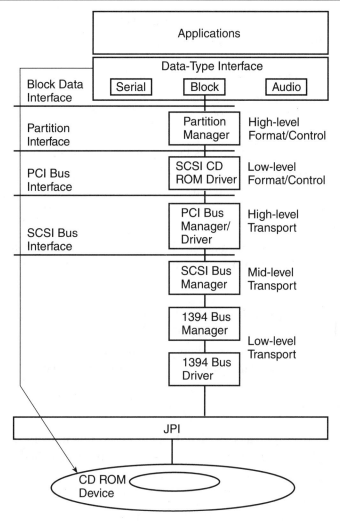

FIGURE 6.5 *SCSI Using a PCI Bus*

(remember, PCI drivers do not have device managers). Otherwise, it is identical to the previous figure in which the SCSI adaptor was connected as a platform device.

6.4 Matching Device Drivers with Bus Drivers

Bus managers discover devices (unless the booter has already done so) and provide device drivers with resources such as memory and interrupt objects. How is a bus driver manager matched to a driver?

The matching process takes place through a simple chain of events beginning with the bus manager and involving both the JSD and the JSL. The matching is accomplished through the following steps:

1. The bus manager detects a previously undetected device on the bus.

2. The bus manager instantiates an inner class whose responsibility is to manufacture memory, interrupt, and possibly other resources for controlling the new device.

3. A reference to this inner class factory object is published in the JSD, causing a device insertion event to be generated by the database.

4. The JSL detects the event, retrieves the bus manager reference from the database, and uses the information it contains to find a driver that matches the new device.

5. The JSL passes the bus manager inner-class reference to the driver. At the same time, the JSL passes the driver a reference to its associated device manager, if any.

The driver now may use the inner-class reference to manufacture memory and interrupt objects that provide access to the device hardware. The driver then interacts with the device through these memory and interrupt objects. The driver also may invoke generic device functions using the reference to its associated device manager.

6.4.1 A Basic Device Driver

A basic device driver is created by first defining a class that implements the `Device` interface. JavaOS contains an abstract class for this purpose called DeviceDriver. All device drivers begin by extending the DeviceDriver class.

```
public interface Device {...}
public abstract class DeviceDriver implements Device {...}
```

Often, the device will belong to a device category for which JavaOS has defined a more specific interface. In these situations, the device driver should extend the more specific category class.

```
public interface ScsiDevice extends Device {...}
public abstract class ScsiDeviceDriver implements ScsiDevice {...}
```

The base class of all device managers is called, appropriately, `DeviceManager`. Device managers are just device drivers with generic functionality. Like device drivers, they implement the `Device` interface:

```
class DeviceManager implements Device {…}
```

For specific device categories, specific manager classes are created:

```
public interface AudioManager extends Device {...}
public abstract class AudioDeviceManager implements AudioManager
{...}
```

That may or may not be where the similarity between a device manager and its driver ends. Sometimes, the manager will implement the same extended interface as the driver; other times, the manager and the driver will implement entirely different interfaces. Incidentally, we have discussed how drivers call the methods of managers to obtain generic device functionality, but there is no reason a manager cannot also call the methods of a driver. All the manager would need is a reference to the driver object, something easily obtained from the JSL.

It is important to understand that a device driver and a device manager are separate objects. A device manager contains common code for the category of devices to which the device driver belongs. A device driver is not an extended class of a device manager. When the driver needs to invoke a common function for its device category, it calls the methods of the device manager.

6.4.2 A Basic Bus Driver

A basic bus driver is created by first extending the base Bus interface. *Bus* defines functionality that is common to both expansion and external I/O buses:

```
public interface Bus {...}
```

The JDI defines two extended interfaces, one for expansion buses, the other for external I/O buses:

```
public interface ExpansionBus extends Bus {...}
public interface IOBus extends Bus {...}
```

The ExpansionBus interface defines expansion bus methods that are independent of a particular expansion bus category. Likewise, the IOBus interface defines I/O bus methods that are independent of a particular I/O bus category.

Finally, methods that are common across a category of expansion or I/O bus are defined with specific interfaces. For example:

```
public interface PCIBus extends ExpansionBus {}
public interface SCSIBus extends IOBus {}
```

Table 6.1 provides examples of bus category interfaces. A bus driver that controlled a particular bus chip set would extend one of these bus category interfaces.

TABLE 6.1 Bus Family Examples

Bus Family	Chip Set	Bus Manager Class	Bus Interface
PCI Expansion Bus	VL82C59x from VLSI Technology	PCIBusManager	PCIBus
ISA Expansion Bus	Intel 380 Dock Set	ISABusManager	ISABus
SCSI I/O Bus	AHA-2940 from Adaptec	SCSIBusManager	SCSIBus
Universal Serial I/O Bus	USBN9602 from National Semiconductor	USBBusManager	USBBus

6.5   The JavaOS Device Interface

The JavaOS Device Interface (JDI) is a collection of classes and interfaces that make the job of writing JavaOS device drivers easier. The Device interface and DeviceDriver class shown in the preceding section are examples of JDI components. The JDI includes classes and interfaces for creating device drivers, device managers, bus drivers, and bus managers. The JDI also contains classes and interfaces for implementing control functions that are common among many categories of devices. These common control functions are called *utility functions*. A good example of a utility function is power management. Many devices implement power management features, regardless of which category they fall under.

The JDI also includes functions for managing different types of data. For example, the JDI includes classes and interfaces for managing character-oriented (streaming) data, block-oriented data, audio data, and video data. These *data-type* functions are specific to data type, not to any particular category of devices. For example, the audio data functions are used to transfer audio data to or from a network adaptor device in realtime. A network adaptor is not a member of the audio device category, but the audio data type interface can be used nonetheless to transfer data to the device. In Figure 6.5, showing the I/O stack for a SCSI CD ROM device, the Partition Manager exported a data-type interface (BlockData) to clients above and communicated with drivers below" using a Partition interface (also a data-type interface).

Figure 6.6 shows the JDI ingredients that go into a typical device driver. For example, a device driver can be declared as:

```
public class MyDeviceDriver extends MyDeviceCategory implements
   PowerManagement, Partition {...}
```

(The device category class MyDeviceCategory implements the device category interface.)

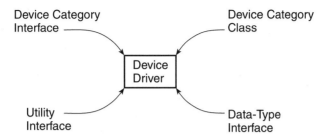

FIGURE 6.6 *Device Driver Ingredients*

These are the ingredients of a device driver. The device driver will also have associated support classes, including the device manager for the driver, a device handle class, event classes, and exception classes.

It is important to understand the distinction between data-type functions and utility functions. Data-type functions are used to manage a data type independently of any device category. Utility functions do not manage data; they are control functions that are common across device categories.

A short "cookbook" on how to create a widget driver includes the following steps:

1. Create the `Widget` interface, extending a current device category interface. If the widget device represents a totally new category of device, extend the generic `Device` interface.

2. Create the widget device-driver abstract class named `WidgetDeviceDriver`, extending the `DeviceDriver` class hierarchy in the same manner as the `Device` interface was extended.

3. Create a set of unique exception classes for the widget device.

4. Create a set of unique event classes and interfaces for the widget device.

5. Create a widget device handle class named `WidgetDeviceHandle`, extending the handle hierarchy in the same manner as the `Device` and `DeviceDriver` hierarchies were extended.

The next section describes the process of creating unique exception and event classes for a device driver.

6.6   Exceptions and Events

Device exceptions are thrown when an error condition occurs. Each exception object contains a reference to the device that was in use when the exception was thrown. The JDI contains some standard exception classes that may be extended by drivers. All of these standard exceptions extend the base `DeviceException` class.

```
public class DeviceException extends Exception
```

The standard JDI exception classes are:

`DeviceAccessException`—thrown when a driver client attempts an
    operation that exceeds the permissions with which the driver was opened

`DeviceInUseException`—thrown when an attempt is made to open a device
    that is already open in exclusive mode

`DeviceAlreadyOpenException`—thrown when a second open is attempted
    on the same open device handle

`DeviceNotOpenException`—thrown when a close operation is attempted on
    a device handle that is not open

`DeviceOpNotSuppException`—thrown when an attempted operation is not
    supported by the device driver

Events are objects that extend the `java.util.EventObject` class. Event listeners extend `java.util.EventListener`. For more details on creating operating system events, see Chapter 3.

6.7   Device Handles

Device handles are objects that serve as a gateway through which clients access the methods of drivers. They also provide a way for clients to query the capabilities of drivers without loading the driver code or instantiating a driver object. Device handles are manufactured by device managers for the category of device to which the driver belongs and returned to the client.

All device handles extend the base `DeviceHandle` class.

```
public abstract class DeviceHandle implements Device,
OSEventConsumer {...}
```

The device handle implements `open()` and `close()` methods which cause the associated device driver object to be instantiated and discarded, respectively. The first `open()` invocation by any client of the driver will cause the driver code to be loaded into memory. The final call to `close()` by the last client of the driver discards the driver code for unloading. Before opening the driver, the client can call `getDeviceActions()` on the handle to determine which functions are supported by the driver.

The list of supported functions (also known as *actions*) will vary according to the permissions of the client. For example, a client with read-only permissions may receive a list of supported functions consisting of a `read()` method even though the driver is capable of writing data as well. The list is returned as a sequence of strings.

When a client invokes an I/O or control method on the handle, the method is passed through to the driver. Before passing along the call, the handle verifies that the client has permission to access that method and if not, throws an exception. The call may be passed through by simply invoking the associated method on the driver, or through more elaborate means, such as using Remote Method Invocation if the driver is running on the server.

Figure 6.7 shows three means (a direct method call, an event, or an RMI method call) by which a device handle may pass through calls to the device driver methods.

An invocation of a driver method can be either *synchronous* or *asynchronous*. Synchronous invocations proceed as a series of method calls from client through handle to driver, all on the same thread. In other words, the driver method runs in the invoking client's thread. This is the situation depicted by the left-most stack in Figure 6.7.

Asynchronous invocations use events to perform a thread switch from client to driver. This is the situation depicted in the middle stack of the figure. The client sends the driver an event object that tells the driver everything it needs to know to fulfill the client's request. Receipt of the event may cause the driver to invoke multiple methods. Once the request is fulfilled, the driver returns any requested information, or merely acknowledges the request by sending an event object back

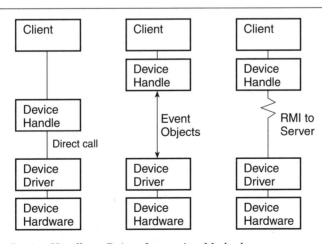

FIGURE 6.7 *Device Handle to Driver Invocation Methods*

to the client. The client and driver execute in different threads, providing more isolation and, hence, protection between drivers and their clients.

The RMI invocation depicted in the right-most stack of Figure 6.7 also is a form of asynchronous invocation because the client runs on a thread on the client machine and the driver runs on a server thread.

6.8   JDI Serial Port Device Example

The JavaOS Comm API (`javax.comm`) implementation is layered upon the JDI. This section describes the JDI `SerialPort` class and interface hierarchies supporting the Java Comm API implementation. For the sake of brevity, the following code samples do not contain any exception definition or handling.

6.8.1   Interfaces

A serial port is a communication device that supports control functions as well as input and output byte streams. All JDI devices are defined in terms of an interface that ultimately extends the `Device` interface. Figure 6.8 illustrates the JDI `SerialPort` interface hierarchy beginning at the `Device` interface and extending to the `SerialPort` interface.

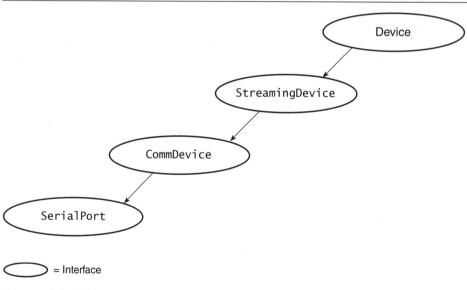

FIGURE 6.8   *JDI* `SerialPort` *Interface Hierarchy*

Device *Interface*

The Device interface defines the basic methods supported by all JDI devices.

```
public interface Device {
    public String[] getDeviceActions();
    public DeviceHandle[] getOpenDeviceHandles();
    public DeviceHandle getCurrentOwner();
    public static final String[] actions = {"getInfo"};
}
```

All devices support actions (a set of related methods) and device handles. The most basic action supported by all devices is getInfo(). The information available from a device includes what actions the device supports and the set of handles associated with the device.

StreamingDevice *Interface*

The StreamingDevice interface defines the basic methods supported by all JDI streaming devices.

```
public interface StreamingDevice extends Device {
    public InputStream getInputStream();
    public OutputStream getOutputStream();
    public void setInputBufferSize(int size);
    public int getInputBufferSize();
    public void setOutputBufferSize(int size);
    public int getOutputBufferSize();
    public static final String[] actions = {"read","write"};
}
```

All streaming devices support read and write actions. Reading from a streaming device is accomplished using an InputStream. The device's input stream is returned to handles opened for "read" by the getInputStream() method.

Writing to a streaming device is accomplished using an OutputStream. The device's output stream is returned to handles opened for "write" by the getOutputStream() method.

The remaining methods control input and output buffer sizes.

CommDevice *Interface*

The CommDevice interface defines the basic methods supported by all JDI communication devices, such as serial and parallel ports.

```
public interface CommDevice extends StreamingDevice {
    public void enableRcvThreshold(int thresh);
    public void disableRcvThreshold();
    public int getRcvThreshold();
    public void enableRcvTimeout(int rcvTimeout);
    public void disableRcvTimeout();
```

```
        public int getRcvTimeout();
        public boolean isRcvTimeoutEnabled();
        public void enableRcvFraming(int framingByte);
        public void disableRcvFraming();
        public int getRcvFramingByte();
        public boolean isRcvFramingEnabled();
        public static final String[] actions = {"control","status"};
    }
```

All communication devices support status and control actions (methods). Status methods return information about the communication device, while control methods set information. The control and status methods defined by the `CommDevice` interface are well-suited to support the Java Comm API (`javax.comm`).

SerialPort *Interface*

The `SerialPort` interface defines additional control and status methods supported by all JDI serial devices.

```
    public interface SerialPort extends CommDevice {
        public int getBaudRate();
        public int getDataBits();
        public int getStopBits();
        public int getParity();
        public void sendBreak(int milliseconds);
        public void setFlowControlMode(int flowControlMode);
        public int getFlowControlMode();
        public void setRcvFifoTrigger(int trigger);
        public void setSerialPortParams(int baudrate, int databits, int
                    stopbits, int parity);
        public void setDTR(boolean dtr);
        public boolean isDTR();
        public void setRTS(boolean rts);
        public boolean isRTS();
        public boolean isCTS();
        public boolean isRI();
        public boolean isCD();
        public static final String[] actions = {"control","status"};
    }
```

Serial port specific control and status methods manage baud rate, the number of data and parity bits, and the status signals from the hardware, such as Data Terminal Ready (DTR).

6.8.2   Classes

The JDI `SerialPort` class forms the basis of all serial port device driver services. The `SerialPort` class is derived from a class hierarchy that begins at `Service` and extends through `SerialPortDriver`. (See Chapter 4 for a discussion of services

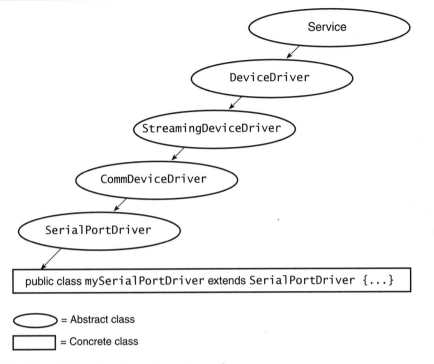

FIGURE 6.9 *JDI* SerialPort *Class Hierarchy*

and the Service class.) The eventual concrete serial driver class must extend SerialPortDriver. Figure 6.9 illustrates the JDI serial port driver class hierarchy.

DeviceDriver *Class*

The DeviceDriver class provides a standard implementation of the methods defined in the Device interface (the getInfo methods) and in the DeviceHandle class (the open and close methods). The DeviceDriver class is defined as follows:

```
public abstract class DeviceDriver extends Service
implements Device {
/* Standard open, close, and getInfo methods */
}
```

StreamingDeviceDriver *Class*

The StreamingDeviceDriver class defines an abstract implementation of the methods defined in the StreamingDevice interface. This class forces a subclass to provide an implementation of StreamingDevice. The StreamingDeviceDriver class is defined as follows:

```
public abstract class StreamingDeviceDriver extends DeviceDriver
implements StreamingDevice {
    public abstract InputStream getInputStream();
    public abstract OutputStream getOutputStream();
    public abstract int getInputBufferSize();
    public abstract void setInputBufferSize(int size);
    public abstract int getOutputBufferSize();
    public abstract void setOutputBufferSize(int size);
}
```

CommDeviceDriver *Class*

The CommDeviceDriver class defines an abstract implementation of the methods defined in the CommDevice interface, forcing a subclass to provide a concrete implementation of CommDevice. The CommDeviceDriver class is defined as follows:

```
public abstract class CommDeviceDriver extends StreamingDeviceDriver
implements CommDevice {
    public abstract void enableRcvThreshold(int thresh);
    public abstract void disableRcvThreshold();
    public abstract int getRcvThreshold();
    public abstract void enableRcvTimeout(int rcvTimeout);
    public abstract void disableRcvTimeout();
    public abstract int getRcvTimeout();
    public abstract boolean isRcvTimeoutEnabled();
    public abstract void disableRcvFraming();
    public abstract void enableRcvFraming(int framingByte);
    public abstract int getRcvFramingByte();
    public abstract boolean isRcvFramingEnable();
}
```

SerialPortDriver *Class*

The SerialPortDriver class defines an abstract implementation of the methods defined in the SerialPort interface, forcing a subclass to provide a concrete implementation of SerialPort. The SerialPortDriver class is defined as follows:

```
public abstract class SerialPortDriver extends CommDeviceDriver
implements SerialPort {
    /* public abstract SerialPort method declarations */
    public abstract .....
}
```

6.8.3 Handles

The JDI implements handles for all standard device categories, including the SerialPort device category. The SerialPort handle is derived from a class hierarchy that begins at DeviceHandle. Figure 6.10 illustrates this portion of the JDI device handle hierarchy and how this class hierarchy is bound by the JSL to a SerialPortDriver during the processing of the open method.

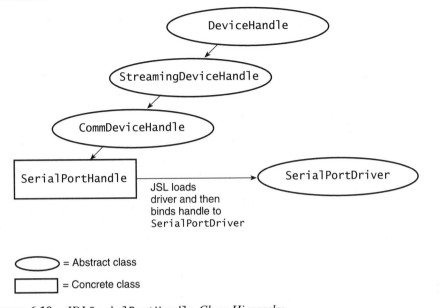

FIGURE 6.10 *JDI* SerialPortHandle *Class Hierarchy*

6.9 Driver Packaging

JavaOS device drivers are loadable on demand. For this reason they must advertise their capabilities to the system so that JavaOS knows which driver to load to fulfill which I/O request. Drivers also must implement interfaces that enable the JSL to load and unload them on demand. These interfaces are described in detail in Chapter 4.

The process of advertising an interface is straightforward. For each interface implemented by a driver, an object called a *service advertisement* is published in the JSD. The JSL can be used to search the database for service advertisements (interfaces) by name. When a suitable match is found, the device driver referenced by the advertisement is loaded and the I/O request fulfilled using the advertised interface.

To be loadable, the driver must implement a standard Service interface. The heart of the Service interface is methods to initialize, finalize, suspend, resume, and manage the driver from the JSL. For complete details on the Service interface, see Chapter 4.

Once a driver's interfaces are advertised, clients can locate drivers by enumerating interfaces by name. For example, to locate a driver for a fax device, the client can invoke the JSL to enumerate all Fax interfaces that have been advertised. The Fax interface advertisements, in turn, contain a reference to the driver that advertised them. Alternatively, clients can take a more direct approach and query the database directly for Fax advertisements. (For a more complete discussion of interface advertisement, see Chapter 4.)

6.10   Summary

JavaOS drivers are either static (included in the boot image) or dynamic. Static drivers cannot be loaded or unloaded without a reboot. Dynamic drivers, by contrast, can be loaded and unloaded on demand, dynamically matched with devices, replaced, and upgraded, all while the OS is running.

JavaOS device drivers are platform-independent, simple to write, and easily managed (as are all JavaOS services) by a system administrator. Although device drivers are platform-independent, they are dependent upon a specific device and bus combination. Device drivers rely on special trusted device drivers that manage buses to provide resources such as memory and interrupt objects.

Device handles are objects through which clients access the methods of drivers. Device handles provide a way for clients to query the capabilities of drivers without loading the driver code or instantiating a driver object.

Chapter 7
Memory

Access to memory is a fundamental operation in any computer system. All software accesses memory in order to store and retrieve data, even when that data is only transient in duration (program variables). It should come as no surprise that the way memory is accessed has a profound effect on the performance and portability of the software in the system.

Addresses describe memory locations. An *address space* is a collection of addresses with similar properties. Address spaces are divided into *memory ranges*, which are subsets of contiguous addresses within the address space. Figure 7.1 illustrates these relationships.

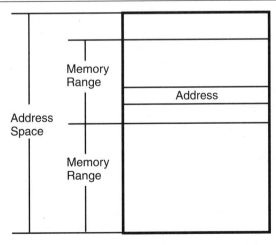

FIGURE 7.1 *Addresses, Address Spaces, and Memory Ranges*

7.1   Memory Basics

The following sections describe the basic organization of memory systems.

7.1.1   Addressing

Addressing is the process of identifying a memory location. The fundamental unit of addressing in JavaOS is the *physical address*. The address translation devices known as memory management units (MMUs) do not translate physical addresses. Rather, a physical address directly identifies a memory location in ROM, RAM, or I/O memory. An address bus provides the physical addresses that initiate the movement of code, data, or both from one platform device to another. Devices acting as bus masters on the address buses generate physical addresses on the address bus.

Bus master devices, such as CPUs, generate addresses. Slave devices, such as framebuffers and simple serial ports, respond to but do not generate addresses. Some devices can both generate and respond to addresses. Code and data move on a data bus when a bus master generates addresses on an address bus.

JavaOS views the CPU as just another device that generates and responds to physical addresses. A memory-mapped bus extends the CPU's view of physical memory to include the devices attached to that bus. General-purpose *load* and *store* instructions can access attached devices called *memory-mapped* devices. Memory-mapped buses include PCI, Sbus, and VME. Not all buses and devices fall into this category, however. Some buses require special instructions to generate an address. For example, the x86 family of processors supports *port addressing*. A port is a physical address generated using special *in* and *out* instructions to the CPU. SCSI is an example of an I/O bus that is not memory-mapped and responds to addresses that identify the bus, device, and logical unit within the device.

Address Spaces

An address space is a range of addressable locations sharing a common set of attributes, such as the size of an address in bits. Each address bus in the system has an implicit associated address space, which consists of the range of addresses the bus can carry.

A *physical address space* is the range of physical addresses that an address bus can carry. The processes and rules governing physical addressing and access are known as *physical memory management*.

A physical address space can contain large ranges of memory that are not actually accessible. Any software attempting to access these "memory holes" is met with a bus error. Most operating systems remove these memory holes from the set of addressable memory using a technique called *virtual addressing*.

Most CPUs (typically with the help of an MMU) support virtual addressing and virtual memory. A virtual address is an abstract identifier of a memory location that must be translated into a physical address before the access occurs. *Virtual memory* is a range of virtual addresses. The total possible range of virtual addresses is called the *virtual address space*.

Another type of address space is the DMA address space. The DMA address space contains the set of physical addresses directly accessible by non-CPU bus masters, such as high-speed network adaptors.

Treating the DMA address space separately from the physical address space allows JavaOS to support DMA controllers with limited addressing capabilities. For example, a 32-bit physical address space may contain a 16-bit DMA address space in the lower half of memory that is accessible to older, 16-bit DMA controllers.

JavaOS supports the concurrent existence of physical, virtual, and DMA addresses in a single system. The microkernel manages all three address spaces. Translation of addresses from space to space is accomplished using a combination of the bus manager interface (see Chapter 6) and the memory classes, which are explained in a later section of this chapter.

Figure 7.2 illustrates the relationship between the physical and virtual address spaces. The shaded portion of the figure represents the virtual address space and

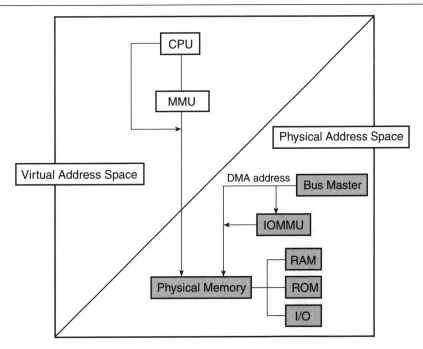

FIGURE 7.2 *JavaOS Address Spaces*

the unshaded portion represents the physical address space. Notice that the only real memory in the system (RAM, ROM, and I/O memory) resides in physical space. Now, notice the arrow descending from the CPU in virtual space to physical space. All software executing on the CPU uses virtual addresses to identify memory locations. When the platform lacks an MMU, software still uses virtual addresses but no translation occurs (physical and virtual memory are identity-mapped). At some point during the CPU's memory access, the virtual address is mapped to a physical address that uniquely identifies a location in physical memory.

When a bus-master device other than the CPU generates an address, the address is treated as a DMA address—even when an I/O MMU is available to translate the DMA address to a physical address or when the DMA and physical address spaces are identity-mapped.

When an I/O MMU is used, a temporary mapping between the DMA and physical address spaces is established. The term of the relationship can be just a single DMA transfer or it can exist for a longer duration. The use of an MMU or I/O MMU to map virtual or DMA addresses to physical addresses is a platform-dependent decision under the control of the microkernel.

7.1.2   JavaOS Address Spaces

Every JavaOS platform supports one physical and one DMA address space. The number of virtual address spaces implemented on a platform depends largely upon the number of concurrent applications required by the product.

At present, network computers and embedded devices running JavaOS require a single application execution model. Theoretically, multiple virtual address spaces can exist, each containing a JavaOS Runtime Environment with its own JVM. Virtual address spaces also can be created to run non-Java (legacy or realtime) software.

7.1.3   Virtual Address Space Usage

JavaOS assigns a virtual address space to a Java application. Assigning an application its *own* address space (separate from the operating system's virtual machine) allows the microkernel to easily track memory allocated on behalf of that application. Assigning each application its own virtual machine also facilitates a simpler application shutdown process. (Shutting down an application is as simple as stopping its virtual machine and removing its address space.) Multiple virtual machines also facilitate features such as background printing. In general, they add to the robustness of the system because each application, virtual machine, and JavaOS Runtime Environment can access memory only within its own virtual address space.

On the other hand, a single virtual address space *shared* by the microkernel and application facilitates a simpler execution model and comprises a smaller memory footprint.[1]

7.1.4 Page Faults

Virtual memory accesses cause a *page fault* when the contents of the underlying physical memory (to which the virtual memory is mapped) are not resident in program memory. Page faults occur only when the virtual address space is larger than the backing physical address space. *Paging*, the process of loading physical memory with the proper contents of a virtual address range, is the job of the microkernel. The JavaOS Runtime Environment manages *heaps,* while the microkernel manages *pages*. Although accesses to physical and DMA memory never cause a page fault, they can cause a bus error (invalid address).

7.1.5 Memory Ranges

The microkernel provides the JavaOS Runtime Environment with a virtual address space. This virtual address space is subdivided into the following contiguous memory ranges:

Microkernel Text Range This is a range of contiguous virtual memory containing the text, native code, of the JavaOS microkernel. This area is read-only. The kernel uses the MMU to enforce the read-only attribute of this range.

Microkernel Data Range This is a range of contiguous virtual memory containing the microkernel's data (uninitialized ".BSS" section of the kernel's load image). This area is read-write and accessed only by the microkernel.

Microkernel Data Heap This range of contiguous virtual memory is for dynamic allocations by native code (`malloc()` and `free()`). This area is read/write. Only the native code portions of the JavaOS Runtime Environment and the microkernel can use memory from this range. This range of memory is not under the control of the garbage collector (GC). It is treated as a pointer-based heap that is managed using a POSIX-style `malloc/free` API.

---

1. The current network computer products from Sun and IBM use a single virtual address space with all system and application code running in the CPU's supervisor (privileged) execution mode. No legacy or real-time code is supported in the current network computer products. The reader should remember that much of the discussion in this chapter presents what the JavaOS memory architecture *supports* as opposed to how a product actually implements the memory system.

Microkernel Stack Range   This range of contiguous virtual memory holds dynamically created thread stacks for native and Java software. Stack space is allocated in page-sized chunks of both a microkernel- and processor-dependent size.

Java Heap Range   This range of contiguous virtual memory holds class objects. This range is patrolled for garbage by the GC. Together, the Java software heap and the microkernel data heap are allocated a fixed range of virtual addresses so that each one grows at the expense of the other or shrinks to the benefit of the other.

Java Method Range   This range of contiguous virtual memory holds the byte codes for methods in the Java programming language. This range is patrolled for garbage by the GC and on some platforms can, in fact, be a part of the Java software heap range. Some versions of JavaOS can collect dead code, others cannot.

Java Constant Pool Range   This range of contiguous virtual memory holds the constant pool tables for all loaded class files.[2]

The JavaOS Runtime Environment creates, manages, and ultimately destroys all Java Runtime Environment areas. The microkernel creates, manages, and destroys all microkernel memory.

Memory ranges are *regions* of an address space. All memory regions have a base address and a length. Each region can subdivide into smaller regions, creating a memory hierarchy. For example, a large virtual-memory region can be allocated from the virtual address space with a base address of 0x00020000 and a length of 0x2000 bytes (8k). The 8k memory region can further subdivide in half or in any other combination of divisions, yielding a hierarchy of memory regions. A bus manager can allocate a single memory region to map a device's register set. The driver subsequently subdivides the register memory into smaller memory regions representing logical groupings of the registers. Figure 7.3 illustrates this concept.

Certain attributes are assigned to memory regions when they are created. Table 7.1 contains the set of these attributes.

The next section explores some common models for accessing memory: the C language model, the C operating system model, the Java programming language model, and, finally, the JavaOS model.

---

2. Separate Java software heap, method, and constant pool memory ranges exist for each active JVM.

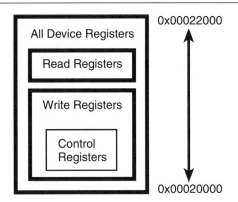

FIGURE 7.3 *Hierachical Memory Regions Mapping Device Registers*

TABLE 7.1 Memory Constraints

Constraint	Result
Minimum valid address	Memory region's lowest address will be >= to this address.
Maximum valid address	Memory region's highest address will be <= to this address.
Allocation alignment mask	Bit mask used to specify region boundary alignment requirements. Constants (representing bit positions in the mask) for page and cache line alignment are provided.
Cache attributes	Region's caching attributes. A memory region can be marked as not-cached, write-through cached, or write-back cached. Unlike the previously discussed attributes, caching attributes can be changed after region creation.
Page residency requirements	The default mode is to allocate pages that are not guaranteed to be resident. However, the micro-kernel can automatically lock the pages in memory and, thus, force resident pages upon region creation.
Access size control	The minimum and maximum access size in bytes. Accesses attempted outside the bounds of specified sizes will force an exception from the memory region.
Access operation control	A region can be marked as read-only or read/write.

7.2   Memory Access Models

The tools available to software for accessing memory locations in the system define the memory access model. The "direct" model provided by the C programming language is one of the more basic memory access models. The C programming language allows software to directly access memory using pointers (variables containing addresses) and pointer (address) arithmetic. This method gives software great power and control over memory. However, the danger is that the software might be poorly designed and might cause damage to other programs or the operating system by manipulating memory locations that other software depends on.

The Java programming language provides a more secure memory access model. The Java programming language eliminates the direct manipulation of memory by eliminating pointers and by providing for the automatic freeing of allocated memory ranges. Eliminating pointers and providing automatic garbage collection makes the Java programming language more robust than C and reduces the number of memory-related bugs.

Most modern operating systems built with the C programming language attempt to confine the memory access of unprivileged software using the CPU's MMU. An access by unprivileged software to memory locations reserved for other software results in a protection fault. A second, "privileged" mode of memory access is provided to trusted software components, such as device drivers. Device drivers are typically executed in the processor's supervisor mode, and the OS programs the MMU to limit I/O memory access (something only drivers should need) to supervisor mode code only. This technique prevents user-mode applications from unsecured memory access but still allows a privileged device driver to crash the operating system with a stray pointer.

JavaOS provides a controlled model for memory access related to the Java language model. The model has enough flexibility, however, to support device drivers, DMA, and other software that must directly access specific addresses or memory ranges. The JavaOS memory access model also makes drivers more portable across JavaOS platforms. This model is *not* part of the Java programming language. JavaOS makes no additions to the language or core classes in order to implement the portable memory model described in this chapter. The next section describes the major features of the JavaOS memory access model.

7.3   The JavaOS Memory Access Model

The philosophy of the JavaOS memory access model can be summed up as follows: encapsulate addresses, address spaces, and memory ranges into classes, and then control access to memory through native methods in those classes. Collectively, these classes are called the *memory classes*.

Looking closer at this simple definition, we see that it reveals many insights into the access model. First, this memory access model works only with the Java programming language, and JavaOS in particular. It is not intended to normalize memory access models on different operating system platforms. Nor is it intended for use by all Java software. For typical memory access operations, such as allocating objects, instance or method variables, or arrays, the Java programming language is perfectly sufficient. However, device drivers written in the Java programming language require low-level memory access to I/O addresses, DMA ranges, or specific addresses, with each access bounds-checked to ensure that it is confined to the regions to which the driver has permission. This is what the memory classes provide.

Second, this model requires the assistance of native methods, which means that some porting is required to implement the JavaOS memory model on different hardware platforms. However, Java software that uses the memory classes does not require porting.

Third, because memory access is accomplished through class objects, the full power of the Java programming language is brought to bear, particularly the use of constructors and garbage collection, greatly simplifying the job of writing device drivers in the Java programming language.

Because memory access is accomplished through method calls, it is CPU- and MMU-independent. From the caller's point of view, the methods work the same regardless of whether the platform implements virtual memory. The caller is shielded from particulars of the address format (the number of bits, byte ordering), and particulars of the CPU data-ordering scheme. *Byte ordering* is the order of bytes (8-bit quantities) within larger words (16-, 32-, and 64-bit quantities). *Data ordering* is the order in which load and store instructions are issued or retired by the CPU.

For example, on systems with out-of-order execution CPUs, the sequence in which store instructions are retired can be reordered from the order in which they are executed. If the destination of the store instructions is addresses in program memory, the CPU ensures that the latest data is written last to any particular RAM location. However, if the destinations are addressed in I/O memory (I/O ports belonging to the same device, for example), then the reordering causes the device to receive the data out of sequence. The memory classes protect against data ordering differences on different platforms.

The native methods have to be fast because they create a level of indirection between the software, which is trying to access memory, and the memory locations themselves. Also, the bounds-checking is typically performed in software. The methods are optimized for speed but even so, memory access using the JavaOS memory classes will not likely be as fast as memory access for the same locations using C pointers and a hardware MMU. This slight performance penalty buys cross-platform portability, and the security and flexibility of a Java software-based memory access model.[3]

To summarize, Java language software that uses the JavaOS memory classes has portable memory access to I/O addresses, DMA, or specific memory-mapped ranges across all JavaOS platforms. The following section explores each memory class in detail.

7.4   Memory Classes

The JavaOS memory access model uses three basic types of memory classes: address classes, address space classes, and memory range classes.

7.4.1   Address Classes

The collection of *address classes* is the fundamental unit of the JavaOS memory-access model. These classes interest both driver and bus manager developers, as well as OEMs porting the OS to a new CPU or microkernel foundation. The address classes define the size and representation of system addresses. They provide a base set of extensible address types that can be used to define more abstract kinds of addresses.

The address class hierarchy begins with a single abstract base class called `Address` and two concrete subclasses, `Address32` and `Address64`, that implement 32-bit and 64-bit addresses, respectively. Figure 7.4 illustrates the hierarchy within the `Address` class.

Class Address
The `Address` base class stores the size of the address in bits and defines abstract methods that must be implemented by the concrete subclasses.

```
public abstract class Address {
    // Package private - the number of bits of this particular
address.
    int bitWidth = 0;

    // Package private constructor.
    Address(int bits)
    {
        bitWidth = bits;
    }
```

---

3. At last count, JavaOS running on a 266MHZ Pentium-2 CPU was able to realize 60 megabits of data throughput on a 100-megabit Ethernet connection.

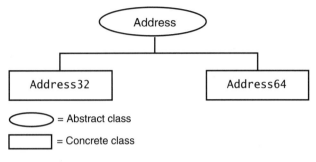

FIGURE 7.4 *Address Class Hierarchy*

```
public int getBitWidth()
    {
        return bitWidth;
    }

    // Representation of this object as a string.
     public abstract String toString();
// Return the value of this Address, casted as an int.
    public abstract int intValue();

    // Return the value of this Address, casted as a long.
    public abstract long longValue();
}
```

The abstract methods support unsigned addition, subtraction, and comparison. In addition, the methods provide for an address conversion to a string, an integer, or a long value.

Class Address32

```
public class Address32 extends Address {
    public Address32(int addrvalue, int bitwidth)
        throws InvalidAddressException
    {...}

    public Address32(int addrvalue)
    {...}

    public Address32(long addrvalue, int bitwidth)
        throws InvalidAddressException {...}
}
```

A 32-bit address can be constructed with an integer or a long value. A bit-width parameter is optional, allowing JavaOS to support addresses smaller than 32 bits. This is important because many 8- and 16-bit devices are still used in embedded platforms. Thus, the Address32 class is really intended for representing addresses *up to* 32 bits in length. The constructor specifies the actual length of the address.

Class **Address64**

```
public class Address64 extends Address {
    public Address64(long addrvalue, int bitwidth)
        throws InvalidAddressException
    {...}

    public Address64(int addrvalue)
    {...}
}
```

A 64-bit address can be constructed with an integer or a long value. A bit-width parameter is optional, allowing JavaOS to support addresses greater than 32 bits and less than 64 bits. (Some versions of the SPARC CPU, for example, support a 36-bit physical address.) The following constructor creates a 36-bit address using the 64-bit address class:

```
long addrValue = 0x0000000208000000;
Address64 thirtySixBitAddr = new Address64(addrValue,36);
```

A constructor throws an InvalidAddressException when an invalid bit width ($< = 32$ or > 64) is specified. The unsigned math operators throw the same exception when an overflow occurs.

7.4.2 Address Space Classes

JavaOS uses an address space class hierarchy to manage memory and aid in the translation of addresses between spaces. JavaOS creates three address space objects (one of each kind) during platform initialization. Figure 7.5 illustrates the hierarchy within the address space class.

Each object in the address space stores the following information:

- Lowest valid address
- Highest valid address
- Name
- ID
- Name of address bus manager

The lowest and highest addresses are always the same size in bits. The name is a string that the address bus manager assigns to the address space. The ID is a 32-bit integer containing a microkernel-assigned ID for the address space.

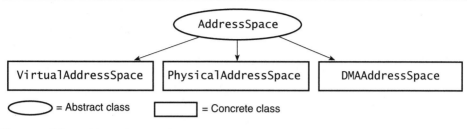

FIGURE 7.5 *Address Space Class Hierarchy*

The class definition of the physical address space provides an illustration of a typical address space:

```
/**
 * Physical Address Space class for JavaOS.
 */

public final class PhysicalAddressSpace extends AddressSpace {
    public PhysicalAddressSpace (ExpansionBus b) {
        super(b, PhysicalAddressSpace.name);
        init(getAddressSize(), alloc_id());
    }

    /**
     * Allocate/map a range of main memory into the physical
     *    address space.
     */
    public native MainMemory allocate(MemoryConstraints c,
        Address len);

    /**
     * Native method to microkernel to get kernel's notion of
     *    address size.
     */
    private native int getAddressSize();

    /**
     * Native method to microkernel to obtain kernel's ID.
     */
    private native int alloc_id();

    public final static String name = "physical";
}
```

7.4.3 Memory Region Classes

The memory region class hierarchy is the most sophisticated of all the memory classes. The Memory class is the base of the memory region hierarchy. This class contains the following information:

- Base address of memory region
- Length of memory region in bytes
- Last address in memory region
- Memory region attributes
- Reference to containing memory region, if any
- Vector of references to contained memory regions, if any

Directly extending the memory class are the `MainMemory`, `MemoryDescriptor`, and `DMAMemory` classes. Objects of type `MainMemory` have the ability to configure the CPU caching attributes for the memory region they define. The `MainMemory` class defines the following cache mode constants to specify caching modes:

```
public static final int CACHE_MODE_DEFAULT=0x0;
public static final int CACHE_MODE_AMBIGUOUS=0x1;
public static final int CACHE_MODE_INHIBITED=0x2;
public static final int CACHE_MODE_WRITE_THROUGH=0x3;
public static final int CACHE_MODE_COPY_BACK=0x4;
```

RAM memory regions are typically cached using the copy-back mode (the highest performance memory caching mode). Copy-back memory access yields the best access times because writes are not flushed to external memory in a synchronous fashion. I/O memory ranges are typically marked "inhibited" (nothing cached by CPU) or "write-through" (lower-performance but fully coherent to external bus masters). Regions marked "ambiguous" contain multiple subregions with differing cache modes.

In addition, the `MainMemory` class defines the following cache management methods that accept and return the cache mode constants:

```
public abstract void setCacheMode(int mode);
public abstract int getCacheMode();
public abstract void flushCache();
```

These methods typically are used by device drivers switching cache modes to either gain increased memory throughput or to make a memory region fully coherent (all contents flushed out of the CPU's cache) with external bus masters.

The `MemoryDescriptor` class represents a region's characteristics, but not its actual allocation. In other words, a `MemoryDescriptor` describes a region's attributes but not its base, ending address, or size. Memory descriptor objects are used by bus managers to describe the attributes of a desired region of memory, but not an allocation. See the bus manager discussion in Chapter 6 for a more complete discussion of memory descriptors.

The `DMAMemoryRegion` class represents information necessary to map a region of physical or virtual memory into the DMA address space. A device driver wishing to initiate a DMA memory transfer must request `DMAMemoryRegion` objects from its bus manager before starting a DMA operation. After the DMA operation is complete, the DMAMemoryRegion object can be discarded at the driver's discretion. Figure 7.6 illustrates the complete hierarchy of memory region classes.

The remainder of the classes in the memory region hierarchy descend from the MainMemory class, beginning with the PhysicalMemory and AccessibleMemory classes. PhysicalMemory describes a region of memory within the physical address space. AccessibleMemory regions represent memory regions that the system CPU directly accesses. The CPU does not directly access physical memory regions; physical addresses must be translated into virtual addresses first. Hence, PhysicalMemory does not descend from AccessibleMemory. Even on systems where virtual addresses are mapped one-to-one with physical addresses (no address translation), JavaOS will not allow direct access of physical memory.

A PhysicalMemory object does not allocate any memory resources. It is merely a descriptor to represent physical memory. This is unlike the VirtualMemory and DMAMemory objects that, when created, result in actual memory allocations.

Memory classes that descend from AccessibleMemory represent memory regions that are programmatically accessible to software. Native methods in these

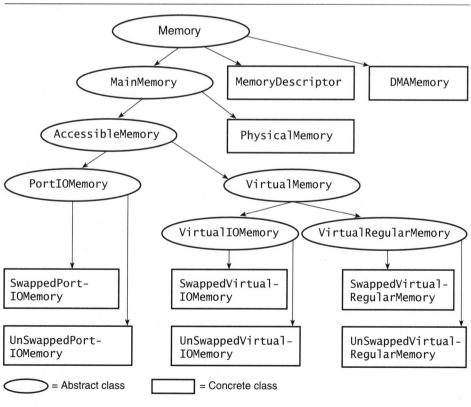

FIGURE 7.6 *Memory Class Hierarchy*

classes read and write to memory locations in these ranges. Range checking prevents access outside the bounds of the region, providing the desired protection from stray references. AccessibleMemory regions are written using the following methods:

```
public void setAddress(int offset, Address value);
public void setByte(int offset, byte x);
public void setShort(int offset, short x);
public void setInt(int offset, int x);
public void setLong(int offset, long x);
public void setBytes(int offset, byte bytes, int bytesOffset,
            int length);
public void setIntArray(int offset, byte bytes, int bytesOffset,
            int length_int);
```

Memory is read from regions using these methods:

```
public byte getByte(int offset);
public short getShort(int offset);
public int getInt(int offset);
public long getLong(int offset);
public void getBytes(int offset, byte bytes, int bytesOffset,
            int length);
public void getIntArray(int offset, byte bytes, int bytesOffset,
            int length_int);
```

Memory may be copied from a source region to a destination region using the following method:

```
public void copy(int offset, AccessibleMemory dest, int destOffset,
            int length);
```

A VirtualMemory object represents a contiguous range of memory within the virtual address space. Virtual memory is either locked or unlocked. Regions placed in the locked state contain resident pages and will not generate page faults. Unlocked regions of virtual memory (the default state) might page, depending upon the implementation of the microkernel. Satisfying page faults is the complete responsibility of the microkernel.

A VirtualMemory object can be constructed in one of three ways:

- Map a set of physical memory ranges (a scatter-gather list) into a contiguous range of virtual memory. This operation may not completely map all the specified physical ranges if the platform doesn't contain an MMU. A successful mapping of physical memory results in a locked virtual memory region, the length of which is the sum of the lengths specified in the scatter-gather list.

- Allocate a region of virtual memory of a specified length. This operation returns an unlocked virtual memory object. Backing physical memory can be assigned immediately, during each page fault, or when the region is subsequently locked. The mechanics of assigning physical memory pages to back the virtual memory region is under the complete control of the microkernel and subject to the limitations of the platform and CPU hardware.

- Allocate a region of virtual memory of a specified length at a specified virtual address. This flavor of virtual memory allocation adds the additional constraint of placing the region at a specified beginning virtual address.

There are two kinds of virtual memory. The first is used to map the I/O space associated with a device attached to an expansion bus such as PCI. Accessing I/O space requires that the accesses are ordered. Some CPUs rearrange memory accesses to optimize performance. Changing the order of access to I/O space can cause unwanted side effects, so the native methods strictly order any access using a VirtualIOMemory object. On the PowerPC CPU chip family, for example, the "eieio" instruction must be inserted in between individual memory accesses to maintain sequential access order.

The second kind of virtual memory object is of type VirtualRegularMemory. These kinds of objects represent regions backed by RAM, which have no special ordering requirements. Hence, native methods do not ensure sequential access.

Memory objects of type PortIOMemory represent regions of memory accessed using special CPU instructions such as "inb" and "outb." Regions of this type accept a port number as an address. The length associated with the region specifies the range of port numbers to be mapped by the memory region.

Instead of using C pointers, special native methods are associated with this kind of region that issue the CPU-dependent instructions to access memory.

Bus managers must determine whether byte swapping is required when accessing memory. Two flavors (swapped and unswapped) of port, virtual I/O, and virtual regular memory are provided to the bus manager for this purpose.

Thus, bus managers always create the following types of memory:

- SwappedVirtualRegularMemory
- SwappedVirtualIOMemory
- SwappedPortIOMemory
- UnswappedVirtualRegularMemory
- UnswappedVirtualIOMemory
- UnswappedPortIOMemory

Native methods defined in each of these classes perform all necessary byte swapping.

7.4.4   Memory Region Creation Using Addresses from the JSD

To enhance the portability of device drivers that must access memory, JavaOS uses a factory model to create memory region objects. Device drivers typically do *not* create their own memory objects. Instead, they build a request for one or more memory objects that map device memory ranges and pass these requests to the device's bus manager. The bus manager looks up certain platform-specific information (such as the CPU address size and the device base address) from the JavaOS System Database and manufactures a compatible memory object. This memory object is returned to the driver, which then uses it to access device memory. Figure 7.7 illustrates this process.

The JavaOS platform robustness also is enhanced by this factory model because only trusted code (bus managers) is allowed to create and distribute memory objects.

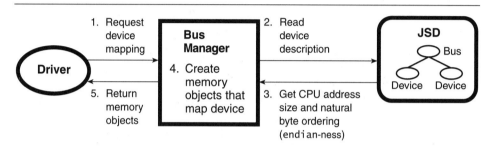

FIGURE 7.7   *Memory Region Creation on Behalf of Device Drivers*

7.5 Summary

JavaOS encapsulates addresses, address spaces, and memory ranges into objects. Memory access is accomplished through native methods in those objects. JavaOS supports the concurrent existence of one physical address space, one DMA address space, and multiple virtual address spaces in a single system.

The JavaOS memory model is not part of the Java programming language. JavaOS makes no additions to the language or core classes in order to implement the portable memory model. For typical memory access operations, such as allocating objects, the Java programming language is perfectly sufficient. However, device drivers written in the Java programming language require low-level memory access to I/O addresses, DMA ranges, or specific addresses. Each memory access is bounds-checked to ensure that it is confined to the regions to which the driver has permission. This is what the memory classes provide.

JavaOS implements a layered memory management architecture. The microkernel occupies the first layer of management and is responsible for address translation, address space protection, and page management.

The runtime memory classes are layered upon the microkernel's page and address space primitives. The proper balance of responsibility between the runtime and microkernel results in a platform-independent memory model that provides the required functionality, security, and performance.

Chapter **8**
Interrupts

JavaOS enables the creation of device drivers that are independent of the platform interrupt mechanism. Abstraction of interrupts is accomplished using classes and interfaces that are part of the JavaOS Platform Interface (JPI). The JPI also contains classes for abstracting the platform memory architecture.

8.1 Abstracting Interrupts

An interrupt is the means by which a device requests attention from software such as a device driver. An interrupt can originate from within the CPU, from a device attached directly to the CPU's external bus, or from a device attached to an expansion bus, such as a PCI bus. JavaOS represents anything that is capable of interrupting with an *interrupt source object.*

Once an interrupt occurs, it requires servicing. Servicing an interrupt involves several steps that usually, but not always, occur in the following order:

1. Disable interrupts from the source so that the source cannot interrupt again during interrupt service.
2. Take appropriate action in response to the interrupt (usually involves reading data from or writing data to the interrupt source).
3. Reenable interrupts from the source.
4. Acknowledge the interrupt with the interrupt controller associated with the source. Acknowledgment enables the interrupt controller to accept new interrupts from the device.

Typically, when a peripheral device generates an interrupt, the interrupt signal propagates over one or more buses until it reaches the associated interrupt controller, which then interrupts the CPU. The interrupt is assigned to a CPU interrupt level, which identifies the interrupt relative to other interrupts and also can identify its relative priority.

The route taken by an interrupt from the source device to the CPU need not always be the shortest route between the device and CPU in the JavaOS System Database (JSD) `Device` tree (see Chapter 2). For this reason, a tree separate from the `Device` tree is used to represent the interconnection of interrupt sources on the platform.

JavaOS creates interrupt source objects to represent the CPU, each CPU interrupt level, and each device associated with an interrupt level. A tree of interrupt source objects represents the interrupt topology (the interconnection of interrupt enabled devices). Figure 8.1 illustrates the interconnection of the CPU, each CPU interrupt level (two in this case), a bus interrupt source, and two device interrupt sources.

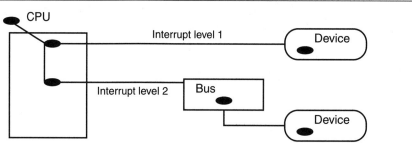

FIGURE 8.1   *Physical Interrupt Topology*

8.1.1   The Interrupt Source Tree

A subtree within the JSD's Interrupts namespace represents the physical interrupt topology of the hardware platform shown in Figure 8.1. This hierarchy is called the Interrupt Source Tree (IST).

The IST is an exclusive feature of JavaOS. The JSD on non-JavaOS platforms, such as Windows or Solaris, does not include the IST because the underlying OS manages interrupts in a platform-dependent manner. Levels of the IST represent the CPU (the tree root), CPU interrupt levels, buses, and, finally, devices (leaf entries). Each platform can require a differently shaped IST to convey the interconnection of interrupting devices.

Figure 8.2 shows the physical interrupt topology from Figure 8.1 as an IST.

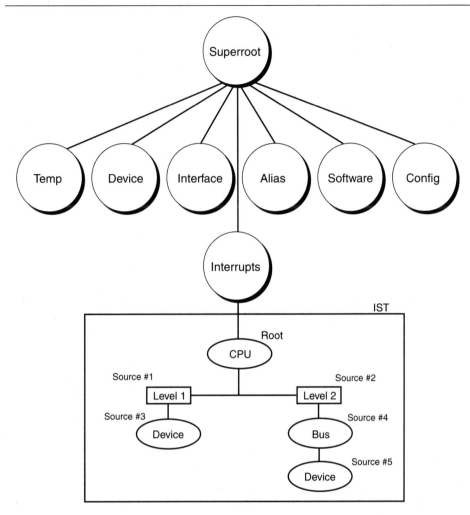

FIGURE 8.2 *Interrupt Source Tree for Figure 8.1*

8.1.2   Interrupt Source Entries

A JSD entry called an Interrupt Source Entry (ISE) represents each interrupt source. ISEs are objects in the Java programming language that both Java software and native code may access, sometimes concurrently. In Figure 8.2, an ISE would represent each component of the IST labeled "source."

An ISE object subclasses the JSD's base `SystemEntry` class:

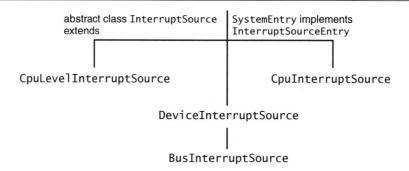

FIGURE 8.3   InterruptSource *Class Hierarchy*

```
import java.system.database.Entry;
public InterruptSourceEntry extends SystemEntry implements
InterruptRegistration {...}
```

The ISE implements an interrupt registration interface consisting of methods that install and remove driver-supplied software components to manage interrupts from a particular source. This chapter discusses these interrupt-management software components in more detail in a later section.

Figure 8.3 illustrates the JavaOS interrupt class hierarchy.

The DeviceInterruptSource class represents ISEs for devices that generate interrupts, and the BusInterruptSource represents a bus interrupt source. A single CPUInterruptSource is used to represent the CPU, and a CpuLevelInterruptSource represents each level of interrupt recognized by the CPU.

When creating an ISE to represent a bus, the maximum number of associated child ISEs must be specified, one for each interrupting device that could attach to the bus. Precreating child "slots" has a number of advantages for the native code that must access an ISE during interrupt servicing. The first advantage is that all memory associated with the bus ISE (including any child ISEs) can be easily locked to prevent page faults. (Most microkernels cannot support the handling of page faults during interrupt processing.)

Second, a bus ISE can store references to device ISEs in a precreated array. Using an array within an ISE allows bus managers to number the child devices and use that number as an array index. This is especially important during interrupt servicing because indexing into an array is much simpler than walking a linked-list or other dynamically managed storage vector.

8.1.3 IST Construction

The IST is built dynamically when JavaOS boots. Constructing the IST is the responsibility of the platform manager (the default system device manager) and each platform bus manager (see Chapter 5). First, the platform manager creates the `Interrupt` namespace root and installs itself as the manager of this namespace. (See Chapter 2 for more information on namespace managers.) Next, the platform manager creates the CPU ISE to serve as the root of the IST and then proceeds to create a child ISE of the CPU ISE for each CPU interrupt level.

Bus managers are matched to bus entries in the `Device` namespace during booting by the device manager. As part of a bus manager's initialization process, entries are added to the IST to represent the interrupting devices on the bus assigned to the bus manager.

Drivers construct interrupt source entry objects and then ask the appropriate bus manager to install the ISE into the IST. The bus manager decides where the new ISE resides beneath it in the tree. The position in the tree is platform-dependent, reflecting the routing of the interrupt from its source to the CPU.

As the device manager matches devices with drivers and buses with bus managers, the IST grows and interrupt management components are registered for each entry. Cross-references between the `Device` and `Interrupt` namespaces are created using a JSD property to cross-reference devices with interrupt sources. Figure 8.4 illustrates cross-referencing of the `Device` and `Interrupt` namespaces.

Figure 8.5 illustrates the software components that manage interrupts at different levels of the IST.

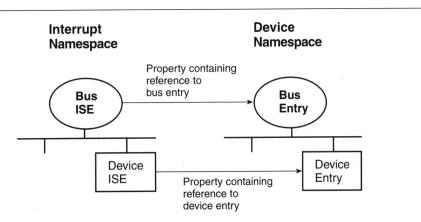

FIGURE 8.4 *Interrupt and Device Namespace Cross-Referencing*

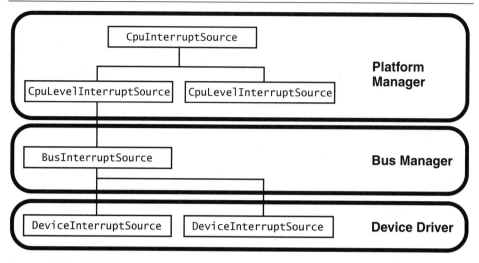

FIGURE 8.5   *IST Management*

8.2   Interrupt Management

For each device capable of generating an interrupt, one or more software components are registered to handle and manage interrupts from the device.

Four kinds of software components can be registered to manage interrupts for an ISE:

- Interrupt enabler
- Interrupt disabler
- Interrupt acknowledger
- Interrupt handler

Interrupt Enabler   An interrupt enabler places the device in a state where interrupts are possible, that is, *unmasked*. A CPU interrupt enabler enables all interrupt levels supported by the CPU interrupt controller. An interrupt-level enabler unmasks only a single interrupt level. A bus or device enabler unmasks only those interrupts from the bus or device.

Interrupt Disabler   An interrupt disabler is like an interrupt enabler, except that it places the device in a state where interrupts are impossible, or *masked*. Like enablers, interrupt disablers are specific to a CPU, an interrupt level, a bus, or a device.

Interrupt Acknowledger An interrupt acknowledger communicates to the interrupt controller the fact that the interrupt has been handled. This is called interrupt acknowledgment. Acknowledgment can take place before or after an interrupt is actually dispatched to a handler. Device drivers never access interrupt controllers directly. Instead, they use the interrupt acknowledger to perform such access.

Interrupt Handler An interrupt handler executes in response to an interrupt. Its job is to satisfy the device's request for attention, read or write any pending data, and return control to the operating system as soon as possible. JavaOS supports three levels of interrupt handlers, as explained in a later section.

8.2.1   Registering Interrupt Code

Software components that implement handlers, enablers, disablers, and acknowledgers must be registered with an interrupt source entry before JavaOS will recognize them. When a new ISE is added to the interrupt software tree, the ISE inherits its parent's registered interrupt management components until code that is specific to the ISE is registered.

Interrupt management components must implement well-defined interfaces. Interrupt enablers implement `InterruptEnabler`. Interrupt disablers implement `InterruptDisabler`, and interrupt acknowledgers implement `Interrupt-Acknowledger`. The next section explains the other interfaces for first-, second-, and third-level interrupt handlers.

Interrupt Management Interfaces

```
public interface FirstLevelInterruptHandler {...}
public interface SecondLevelInterruptHandler {...}
public interface ThirdLevelInterruptHandler {...}
public interface InterruptEnabler {...}
public interface InterruptDisabler {...}
public interface InterruptAcknowledger {...}
```

The ISE class defines a number of get/set methods to register interrupt code. For example:

```
public ThirdLevelInterruptHandler
getThirdLevelInterruptHandler();
public void
setThirdLevelInterruptHandler(ThirdLevelInterruptHandler ih);
```

8.2.2   Interrupt Handlers

JavaOS recognizes three interrupt handling levels, each level defining a handler and an execution context for that kind of handler. The microkernel implements two of the three interrupt levels in native code. Third-level interrupt handlers are implemented in the Java programming language.

Each handler level runs in its own execution context. A single interrupt source can have all, some, or no handler levels registered to process interrupts.

Handlers at one level can communicate state and data to handlers at any other level using the interrupt source entry as a common data exchange point.

Two of the interrupt processing levels are deferred, meaning a thread switch occurs between the time the interrupt occurs and the time the interrupt is handled. A deferred interrupt level is always triggered from native code by a first-level interrupt handler.

The three interrupt levels, explained in Table 8.1, are:

- First-level realtime native interrupt level
- Second-level deferred native interrupt level
- Third-level deferred interrupt level

The Need for Native Interrupt Handlers

All Java software executes in the context of a Java software thread. Java software thread scheduling is periodically disabled whenever the virtual machine's garbage collector runs to clean up heap memory. Due to the garbage collector's current "mark and sweep" algorithm, the amount of time that the garbage collector requires increases linearly as the size of the Java software heap increases. Disabling Java software thread scheduling for long periods of time presents a problem for interrupt handlers written in the Java programming language. It is possible that the handler will not run soon enough after an interrupt occurs to prevent the loss of device data.

Native interrupt handlers can preempt the garbage collector, providing realtime response to device interrupts. Devices that present large amounts of data (and

TABLE 8.1   Interrupt Levels

	1st Level	2nd Level	3rd Level
Deferred	No	Yes	Yes
Code	Native	Native	Java software
Context	Interrupt	Kernel thread	Java software thread

do so with a high number of interrupts) are candidates for native interrupt handlers. Devices using serial, parallel, or Universal Serial Bus (USB) communication buses, for example, use native interrupt handling to prevent data loss. Figure 8.6 illustrates the range of devices best suited to native interrupt handling.

First-Level Handler

First-level interrupt handlers are native interrupt handlers that execute at the CPU's interrupt level. First-level handlers are composed of native code that obeys the C calling conventions defined for the processor, even if the handler is written in assembly language. First-level interrupt handlers are necessary when a device might lose data if its interrupts are not serviced in a timely fashion. The execution duration of a first-level interrupt handler should be on the order of hundreds of microseconds or less.[1]

Before entering a first-level handler, the microkernel saves processor registers and may switch to a separate interrupt stack. The microkernel determines the stack on which to run first-level handlers. Many microkernels dedicate one interrupt stack per CPU for this purpose. Others will execute the handler on the stack of the current native thread.

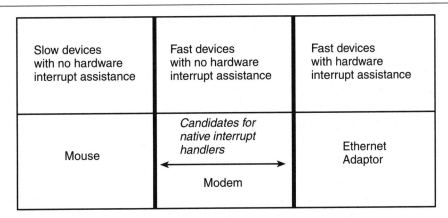

FIGURE 8.6 *Device Types and Native Interrupt Handling Recommendations*

---

1. In early releases of JavaOS, all native interrupt handlers are linked into the platform and cannot be dynamically loaded from the network or a disk. Future versions of JavaOS might allow for native code loading. It is even conceivable that a Just-In-Time (JIT) compiler could dynamically generate native interrupt handlers some day.

A first-level interrupt handler can:

- Read and write data within the interrupt source object for the interrupt.
- Traverse the IST.
- Identify and invoke other first-level interrupt handlers.
- Signal an ISE object so that waiting threads in second- or third-level interrupt handlers run.

A first-level handler's job is to satisfy the immediate realtime needs of an interrupting device, such as reading data from a device with limited buffering capability. After satisfying the realtime needs of a device, a first-level interrupt handler may cause a second- or third-level handler to be queued for execution. A first-level handler can pass state, data, or both to deferred second- and third-level handlers. This is done through the interrupt source object to get and set data within the object.

The handler returns an integer that signals whether the interrupt was processed by the handler. The following listing shows the declaration of a native first-level interrupt handler[2]:

```
#include <sun_javaos_InterruptSource.h>
int sun_javaos_InterruptSource_handleFirstLevelInterrupt(struct
Hsun_javaos_InterruptSource *ise, long when) {
}
```

The first parameter to the handler entry point is a C pointer to the invoking ISE object. The second parameter is the lapsed time since system boot, in microseconds.

First-level interrupt handlers are the highest-priority code in the system, preempting other interrupt handlers and threads. Consequently, the processing time spent in a first-level interrupt handler should be kept to a minimum.

Second-Level Handler

A second-level interrupt handler runs in the context of a native kernel thread. Like the first-level handler, the second-level handler also is composed of native code that obeys the C calling conventions and is prototyped in the Java programming language as a native method with a single parameter. Second-level interrupt handlers are useful for extended realtime processing, such as that required by multimedia applications.

---

2. Multiple first-level interrupt handlers can execute simultaneously, each at a different CPU interrupt level. This is true in a single CPU and also in a Symmetric Multi-Processing (SMP) system. In a SMP system, however, the microkernel serializes the execution of each CPU interrupt level so that two CPUs do not attempt to execute the same handler simultaneously.

Like a first-level handler, a second-level handler has a limited number of support services at its disposal. Native handlers (first and second levels) can get and set ISE data and to invoke other native methods associated with the same ISE.

A second-level interrupt handler executes under two circumstances. A first-level interrupt handler can queue a second-level handler. If no first-level handler exists, the microkernel automatically queues the second-level handler in response to an interrupt.

The following listing shows the C declaration of a native second-level interrupt handler:

```
#include <sun_javaos_InterruptSource.h>
int sun_javaos_InterruptSource_handleSecondLevelInterrupt(struct
Hsun_javaos_InterruptSource *ise, long when) {
}
```

The microkernel creates a native thread to execute the second-level handler. Second-level interrupt handlers have a lower priority than first-level interrupt handlers but can preempt third-level handlers and other Java or native threads.

Third-Level Handler

A third-level interrupt handler runs in the context of a typical Java software thread and, therefore, can use the full resources of the Java programming language and the JavaOS Runtime Environment. Third-level interrupt handlers are useful for nonrealtime processing, such as mouse and keyboard event handling. Third-level interrupt handlers might experience sporadic latencies due to interruption by the virtual machine's garbage collector. If these latencies are unacceptable for a particular device, a second- or first-level interrupt handler should be used.

If no first- or second-level handler is registered for an interrupt source object, the microkernel queues the third-level handler for execution when the device interrupts. Also, either a first- or second-level handler can queue a third-level interrupt handler. Third-level interrupt handlers have a lower priority than either first- or second-level interrupt handlers.

8.2.3 Synchronizing Interrupt Handlers

With multiple levels of interrupt handling comes the problem of synchronization. JavaOS allows a driver's noninterrupt-level code to synchronize with all three levels of interrupt handlers.

As an example, consider the synchronization of a driver with second- and third-level interrupt handlers. Threads that execute second- and third-level handlers acquire the Java software monitor associated with the ISE *before* executing the handler. Thus, a driver can block a second- or third-level handler from executing by acquiring the ISE's monitor. If an interrupt handler is already executing, the driver will block until the handler releases the monitor. If the monitor is free, the driver will acquire the monitor and prevent any subsequent monitor acquisition attempt by a handler, blocking execution of the interrupt handler until the driver releases the monitor.

Synchronizing with code not executing within a thread context (that is, first-level interrupt handlers) requires that the driver enable and disable the interrupt source itself. Each ISE object implements an interface that contains methods for this purpose. Disabling the interrupts prevents any further invocations of the first-level handler. If the handler is executing at the moment when an interrupt disables, the handler completes execution and does not invoke again until the interrupts are reenabled and an interrupt occurs. Figure 8.7 shows the processing of an interrupt from the time the device raises the interrupt to the time that all three levels of interrupt handlers dispatch.

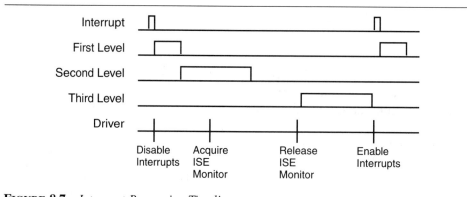

FIGURE 8.7   *Interrupt Processing Timeline*

8.2.4   Queuing a Deferred-Interrupt Handler

Native first-level and second-level interrupt handlers can choose to defer interrupt processing until a later time on a per-interrupt basis. To defer work from a lower-level handler to a higher-level handler, an interrupt handler *notifies* the current interrupt source object. Notifying the interrupt source object causes the microkernel to wake up interrupt handler threads that are waiting to process the interrupt.

For example, a third-level interrupt handler runs in the context of a precreated thread. The waiting thread maintains a loop that looks something like this:

```
public class InterruptThread {
    public synchronized void waitForInterrupt() {
    boolean interrupted = false;
```

```
        while(1) {
            try { wait(); } catch (InterruptedException ex) {
    interrupted = true; }
                }
            }
        }
    }
```

JavaOS automatically defers interrupt processing to higher interrupt levels when no lower-level handler is installed. Figure 8.8 shows a first-level handler notifying the ISE and then ending. The second-level handler then processes the interrupt in a deferred manner.

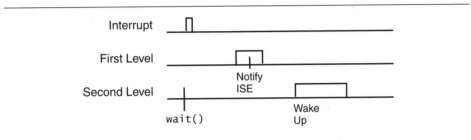

FIGURE 8.8   *Deferred-Interrupt Handling*

8.3   Interrupt Dispatching

Dispatching an interrupt to the appropriate interrupt handler requires native code access to the IST. The IST is made accessible to the native methods of the CPU ISE object during platform initialization. The native methods of this object make sure that each entry in the IST (each object in the Java programming language) is locked down (nonmoveable, page-locked) in the Java software heap. A pointer to the ISE, representing the CPU, is stored in a static variable. When called upon to dispatch an interrupt, the JavaOS interrupt dispatcher accesses this static variable.

8.3.1   Interrupt Dispatcher

The JavaOS interrupt dispatcher is a component of native code that executes first- and second-level interrupt handlers. The native interrupt dispatcher has access to the IST; from here it determines which handlers are registered for which levels.

The interrupt dispatcher is layered upon the microkernel and actually registers itself as a handler of all interrupt vectors that the microkernel exports. Figure 8.9 shows the interrupt dispatcher layered upon the microkernel.

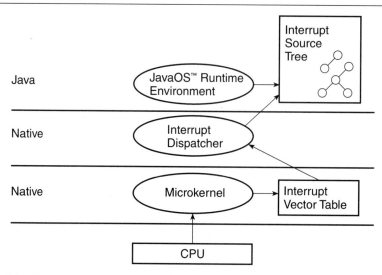

FIGURE 8.9   *Interrupt Dispatcher*

The microkernel has no knowledge of the IST. The interrupt dispatcher reads the IST, figures out which handlers are assigned to which levels, and then presents itself to the microkernel as the sole handler of all interrupts. This design asks little of an underlying microkernel besides a simple interface to install and remove interrupt handlers.

A simple microkernel has only to support a function such as the following C call to support the interrupt dispatcher:

```
int (*native_handler)(int level), void *arg, void *info)
void set_native_intr_handler(int level, native_handler func);
```

The "level" parameter designates a CPU interrupt level (or vector). The "func" parameter designates a native interrupt handler. In passing, a null handler asks the microkernel to remove the handler for a particular level. When an interrupt occurs at the registered level, the microkernel passes control to the handler registered for that level with the current interrupt level as a parameter. The parameters to the interrupt handler itself are explained in the next chapter.

8.3.2   Bus and Device Interrupt Handling Roles

Each bus and each device that can generate an interrupt has an associated interrupt handler. Bus interrupt handlers perform a special decoding function that augments the dispatch logic used by the interrupt dispatcher.

A bus handler determines which device interrupt handler to invoke for a particular interrupt on the associated bus. The bus interrupt handler then invokes the device interrupt handler. In the case of layered buses, multiple bus interrupt handlers can be invoked to decode an interrupt. Eventually a device handler is invoked that actually processes the device's interrupt.

Bus and device interrupt handlers can exist at any of the three levels of interrupt handling, depending upon platform requirements and performance considerations. Regardless of the handler level, the process is always the same. Bus interrupt handlers determine the source of the interrupt on a particular bus. Device interrupt handlers process the interrupt. The only difference at each level is the execution context: interrupt or thread, native or Java software.

Figure 8.10 illustrates the interaction between the bus and device interrupt handlers.

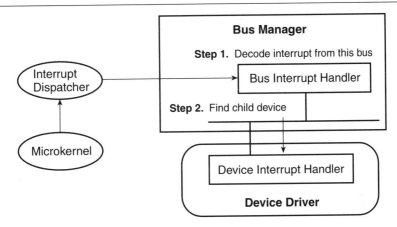

FIGURE 8.10   *Three-Step Interrupt Processing*

8.4   Summary

JavaOS supports three levels of interrupt processing, each with its own execution context:

- First-level native realtime (indeterminate context)
- Second-level (native software thread context)
- Third-level (Java software thread context)

First-level interrupt handlers are preemptive high-priority code that executes in the interrupt context. First-level handlers can schedule (not call) second-level handlers, which will execute in the context of a native kernel thread when the scheduled time arrives. If no first-level handler exists for an interrupt level, the microkernel will automatically queue a second-level handler (if one exists) in response to an interrupt.

Second-level interrupt handlers run in the context of a high-priority native thread and have a lower priority than first-level interrupt handlers, Second-level interrupt handlers preempt third-level handlers and any other Java software or native threads.

A third-level interrupt handler runs in the context of a Java software thread and therefore, may use the full resources of the Java programming language and the JavaOS Runtime Environment. Third-level interrupt handlers may experience sporadic latencies due to interruption by the virtual machine's garbage collector.

Chapter 9
The Microkernel

The microkernel is the bedrock in the layered architecture of JavaOS. It provides basic services to the Java Virtual Machine (JVM) and to the JavaOS Platform Interface (JPI).

No microkernel services are directly available to any native code that is not associated with the JVM, the JPI, or the microkernel itself. Specifically, the microkernel does not directly support native device drivers and native applications.

This chapter explores the microkernel's architecture, its service interface, and the algorithms used to manage the JVM, threads, memory, and more.

9.1 Microkernel Overview

The JavaOS microkernel provides direct services to only two clients: the JVM and the native methods of the JPI. Consequently, the microkernel's architecture and its services are very specific.

A microkernel focused on so few clients has the advantage of simplicity over a general-purpose microkernel that must serve the needs of multiple, diverse clients. Such a simple microkernel is more easily ported, tuned, and maintained. Figure 9.1 illustrates the microkernel and its clients.

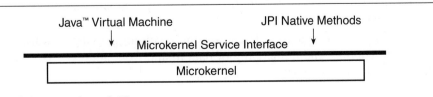

FIGURE 9.1 *Microkernel Clients*

The JavaOS microkernel is designed with the principles described in the following sections in mind.

9.1.1 Run All Software in Supervisor Mode

Many general-purpose microkernels run most software in user mode and reserve the privileged supervisor mode for trusted code and for the microkernel itself.

Each time a microkernel service is invoked, an expensive transition from user to supervisor mode must be executed. Large server operating systems, such as Solaris, have highly optimized paths from user to supervisor mode. The JavaOS microkernel dispenses with the entire requirement, however, choosing instead to run all software (applications and system services) in supervisor mode.

This choice is possible because software written in the Java programming language adheres to the security model for the Java programming language, yielding secure code that cannot crash the microkernel, device drivers, or the virtual machine.

9.1.2 Run All Software in a Single Virtual Address Space

Because the microkernel relies on the Java programming language and the JVM's security model to provide a secure software environment, the microkernel has no need to segregate untrusted software in multiple address spaces.

Most general-purpose microkernels segregate each application into its own address space, preventing the application from crashing the operating system or interfering with the execution of other applications.

The percentage of code that is in a general-purpose microkernel for managing multiple address spaces represents a significant percentage of the total microkernel code. Furthermore, a significant percentage of code in device drivers handles clients from multiple address spaces. Often it is the most complex portion of the driver. This code is absent from JavaOS.

9.1.3 No Inter-Process Communication Service Is Necessary

A microkernel that does not support multiple address spaces has no need for an Inter-Process Communication (IPC) facility. An IPC is typically the communication mechanism of choice for applications and system software operating in a multiple-address-space environment.

The cost and complexity of sending and receiving messages as well as the necessary mapping and unmapping of data to and from address spaces is completely avoided in the JavaOS microkernel.

9.2   Microkernel Architecture

The microkernel architecture recognizes two major programming interfaces and several managers that implement and use these interfaces. Figure 9.2 illustrates these components.

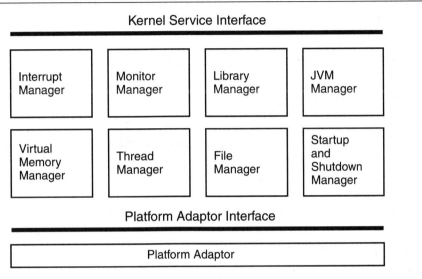

FIGURE 9.2   *Architecture Diagram*

9.2.1   Microkernel Interfaces

Of the two microkernel interfaces, the clients (both external and internal to the microkernel) use one and the microkernel itself uses the other.

Kernel Service Interface

The Kernel Service Interface *(*KSI) is the public interface for external clients of the microkernel. The KSI consists of a set of entry points that, when invoked, causes the microkernel to perform a service and return results. The microkernel's internal components also use this same interface to request services of each other.

The KSI typically is packaged as a library of C functions that are bound with the microkernel's clients either at runtime or, more likely, at build time. The KSI binding largely depends on the product makeup and build-complexity considerations.

Platform Adaptor Interface

The Platform Adaptor Interface (PAI) is a private microkernel interface that binds the microkernel's platform-independent code to the microkernel's platform-dependent code (including the booting system). The platform-dependent code then can be packaged as a pluggable platform adaptor. A platform adaptor provides very low-level services, such as thread context switching and interrupt-level manipulation. The microkernel is always statically bound to the platform adaptor at build time.

Thus, the process of porting the microkernel to a new CPU platform reduces to the implementation of a new platform adaptor.

9.2.2 Microkernel Managers

The microkernel managers, sandwiched between the KSI and the PAI, are a series of platform-independent components that implement the KSI. They also oversee the startup and shutdown procedures of the operating system. The startup and shutdown manager uses the KSI and the PAI to perform its work. The platform adaptor calls the booting system using the JavaOS Boot Interface (JBI). (See Chapter 10 for details.) The remaining managers use the PAI to abstract the platform and use the KSI to implement cross-manager dependencies.

Interrupt Manager

The interrupt manager implements services to register and unregister native interrupt handlers. A native interrupt handler is a C subroutine that executes in response to an interrupt. The process of registering a native interrupt handler causes the C subroutine to be associated with a CPU interrupt level.

The interrupt manager also contains an interrupt dispatcher to process interrupt requests propagated up from the platform adaptor. The interrupt manager can associate multiple interrupt handlers with any one CPU interrupt level.

Virtual Memory Manager

The virtual memory manager (VMM) implements services to map and unmap pages of virtual memory, requesting backing physical pages in the process. Other microkernel managers, the JPI native methods, and the JVM use pages of virtual memory to build higher-level, more fine-grained memory management services.

The VMM relies on the platform adaptor to supply physical pages to back virtual pages. The platform adaptor manages physical pages and any associated external storage, such as a disk, while the memory manager maps and unmaps virtual memory at the request of microkernel clients. The platform adaptor's physical memory manager (PMM) handles page faults, if any.

The VMM also contains a set of memory functions that operate on variable-length byte-sized chunks of virtual memory. These functions layer above the VMM's page management code to provide the JVM with a simple pointer-based memory allocator.

Thread Manager

The thread manager implements services to create, delete, start, stop, suspend, and resume threads. Most threads will execute Java software under the supervision of the JVM. A small portion of threads remains completely native and processes low-level events, such as timer alarms and second-level native interrupt handlers.

The thread manager also manages time on behalf of threads, maintaining a time-ordered list of waiting threads.

Finally, the thread manager contains a set of default native exception handlers. The page fault exception handler, for example, automatically invokes the PMM to satisfy a fault.

Monitor Manager

The monitor manager implements the primitives that form the backbone of Java programming language synchronization. Monitors guard critical sections of Java source code, such as those within a synchronized method. This manager provides services to initialize, enter, and exit monitors.

Library Manager

The microkernel's library manager provides dynamic native code linking at the request of the JVM. The library manager's services include functions that construct library names, load libraries, unload libraries, and find code symbols within a library.

JVM Manager

The microkernel's JVM manager starts and stops the JVM, working to control native mode access to the virtual machine. The JVM manager also supplies a set of system properties to the virtual machine containing information such as the operating system's name, version, and underlying CPU architecture.

File Manager

The file manager contains a native bootstrap file system and a switch to dispatch other Java software file systems that reside in the runtime layer of the JavaOS Runtime Environment. The bootstrap file system contains files (classes, native libraries, and so on) supplied to the startup manager during the booting process.

The number and type of files placed in the bootstrap file system are product-
and platform-dependent. The JVM relies on the FM to find a file. It does not care
if the file resides in the bootstrap file system or in some other file system in the
JavaOS Runtime Environment.

Startup and Shutdown Manager

A component called the start up manager houses the microkernel's startup and
shutdown procedures. This manager contains the microkernel's one-time initialization code, including the code that uses the JBI to obtain booting information
and the contents of the file manager's bootstrap file system.

This manager also contains special code to stop the microkernel and restart
the booting process using a shortcut procedure called "quick reboot." The quick
reboot procedure is useful in many products containing JavaOS because it allows
for faster booting and avoids boot storms, which occur when large numbers of clients boot all at once.

The remainder of the chapter describes the services exported by each manager. The following common C language data types are used throughout this discussion:

```
typedef unsigned long long uint64_t; //64 bit unsigned quantity
typedef unsigned long uint32_t; //32 bit unsigned quantity
typedef long long int64_t; //64 bit signed quantity
typedef long int32_t; //32 bit signed quantity
```

9.3   Interrupt Manager Services

The interrupt manager associates interrupt handlers with a CPU interrupt level, a
process called *interrupt handler registration*. Each CPU interrupt level is defined
as a positive interrupt value. The platform adaptor provides the range of valid
interrupt levels to the interrupt manager.

The following C function prototype defines a native interrupt handler:

```
typedef int (*intr_handler_t)(int interrupt_level, void *arg,
void *info);
```

A native interrupt handler accepts three parameters when dispatched. The first
parameter is an integer containing the current interrupt level. Passing the interrupt
level to the handler allows the same handler to register itself at multiple interrupt
levels.

The second parameter to the interrupt handler is an argument provided to the
kernel at the time of handler registration. The registration argument is typically used
to give the handler a data area from which to read and write during interrupt handling.

The third parameter to the interrupt handler is a platform-dependent argument containing the program counter at the time the platform adaptor receives the interrupt. This information is useful for profiling the operating system.

A native interrupt handler returns an integer-result code that indicates a status to the interrupt dispatcher.

9.3.1   Interrupt-Level Execution Context

A native interrupt handler is subject to several execution constraints. It executes using the current thread stack and in the CPU's native supervisor-mode interrupt level. It cannot block, nor can it yield the CPU to a thread or to another interrupt handler. It cannot allocate or free memory and it can call interrupt-safe routines only within the microkernel manager or the platform adaptor.

9.3.2   Interrupt Processing

Each time a CPU raises an interrupt request, the platform adaptor calls a specially designated subroutine in the interrupt manager. The current interrupt level and the program counter of the current thread pass to the interrupt manager.

Using the interrupt level as an index, the interrupt manager finds the list of interrupt handlers registered at the current interrupt level.

Next, the interrupt manager iterates through the list of handlers, invoking each with the handler's original registration parameter as well as the current interrupt level and program counter. The return value from the handler is checked for a success or failure status.

If the handler returns a value of 1, the interrupt manager assumes the interrupt was handled successfully. A return value of 0, on the other hand, indicates that another handler must be found to process this interrupt. If no handler successfully processes the interrupt, the microkernel logs an error.

9.3.3   Clients of the Interrupt Manager

Two interrupt manager clients exist. Both of these clients are composed of native code residing beneath the JPI. Figure 9.3 illustrates these clients.

Thread Manager

The microkernel's thread manager is the first client of the kernel's interrupt services. The thread manager processes a clock-tick interrupt to keep track of time on behalf of a special clock thread and any other blocked threads that may need to be awakened after a designated maximum time.

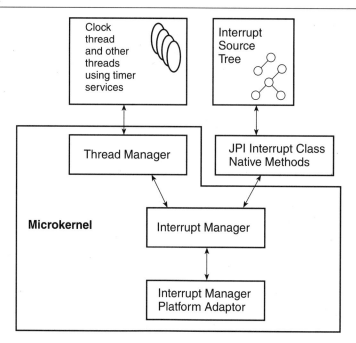

FIGURE 9.3   *Interrupt Manager Clients*

JPI Native Interrupt Methods

The native JPI interrupt methods form the second client of the interrupt manager. These native methods register native interrupt handlers that pass interrupts to native threads and to Java software threads registered in the IST.

The JPI's interrupt management classes implement a more powerful set of interrupt registration and processing abstractions that layer upon the basic services of the interrupt manager. (See Chapter 8 for more details on interrupt management.)

Interrupt Dispatch Logic

The interrupt manager processes native interrupts using the following logic:

1. Wait for an interrupt
2. Determine the level of the highest-priority interrupt
3. Raise the interrupt mask to the current level
4. Dispatch the list of native interrupt handlers

It is the responsibility of the native interrupt handler or a waiting device driver's Java software interrupt handler to clear the device condition that caused the interrupt.

9.4   Thread Manager Services

The thread manager provides a set of threading services tuned to the requirements of the JVM. The services include the following:

- Initialization
- Destruction
- Scheduling
- Information
- Stack management
- Software interrupt and exception management
- Thread management clients

The thread manager uses the following C data type to track a thread's life cycle and context:

```
typedef struct sys_thread sys_thread_t;
```

When the virtual machine needs to specify a thread, the ID (of type `sys_thread_t`) is used as the token that uniquely identifies the thread.

9.4.1   Initialization

The initialization services fall into two subcategories: one-time-only and per-thread. The startup procedure uses two one-time-only thread initialization services.

The startup procedure creates the first thread by using a service that converts the current execution context into a thread. To create the first thread, the startup procedure calls the following service:

```
int sysThreadBootstrap(sys_thread_t *);
```

The output of this service is the ID of the first thread. Once the startup procedure creates the first thread, it executes a method to initialize the rest of the special microkernel threads. Special microkernel thread initialization activates when the startup procedure calls the following service:

```
void sysThreadInitializeSystemThreads(void);
```

The special threads created during microkernel start-up include a clock thread, an idle-time thread, a finalization thread, and an asynchronous garbage collection thread.

The following are the per-thread initialization services:

```
int sysThreadCreate(long, uint_t flags, void *(*)(void *),
sys_thread_t *);
void sysThreadInit(sys_thread_t *);
int sysThreadAlloc(sys_thread_t *);
int sysThreadFree(sys_thread_t *);
```

The `sysThreadCreate` service creates a suspended thread. The first parameter to this service indicates the desired thread stack size. The second parameter contains flags indicating whether this thread is a special thread or a Java software thread. Special threads (like microkernel threads) enjoy some benefit, such as running at higher priorities than Java software threads can.

The third parameter to `sysThreadCreate` contains the thread's initial program counter. The final parameter is an output variable that will contain the ID of the new thread.

The JVM calls the `sysThreadInit`, `sysThreadAlloc`, and `sysThreadFree` services to do preexecution initialization of the stack, and to allocate or free microkernel-specific thread resources.

9.4.2 Destruction

A single thread destruction service is defined as follows:

```
void sysThreadExit(void);
```

The currently executing thread terminates when the JVM invokes this service. Sometimes the JVM invokes this service as the result of an abnormal condition, such as an unhandled exception.

Usually, threads terminate on their own at a time designated by the owning program's logic. Any microkernel resources allocated to the thread are reclaimed at the time of termination.

9.4.3 Scheduling

Quite a few of the thread manager services provide the JVM with thread scheduling control. The thread scheduling services are defined as follows:

```
sysThreadYield(void);
sysThreadSuspend(sys_thread_t *);
sysThreadResume(sys_thread_t *);
sysThreadSingle(void);
sysThreadMulti(void);
```

Those services defined to accept a thread ID operate on any designated thread. The remaining services operate only on the currently executing thread.

Yielding the CPU in a cooperative round-robin fashion (nonpreemptive) is accomplished when the currently executing thread invokes the `sysThreadYield` service at the direction of the JVM. The thread manager also can suspend and resume threads. Suspended threads are not eligible to execute until resumed.

The remaining two services (`sysThreadSingle` and `sysThreadMulti`) operate on the current thread and the thread scheduler. Invoking `sysThreadSingle` causes the thread schedule to lock in the current thread and not allow any other thread to gain control of the CPU.

Threads that use this service should always issue a matching `sysThreadMulti` service call to place the scheduler back into its normal dispatch algorithm.

9.4.4 Information

Various kinds of information can be obtained and changed on a per-thread basis. The following are informational thread services:

```
sys_thread_t * sysThreadSelf(void);
int sysThreadGetPriority(sys_thread_t *, int *);
int sysThreadSetPriority(sys_thread_t *, int);
long * sysThreadRegs(sys_thread_t *, int *);
int sysThreadEnumerateOver(int (*)(sys_thread_t *, void *), void *);
void sysThreadDumpInfo(sys_thread_t *);
int sysThreadSizeof();
int32_t sysThreadCPUTime();
int sysThreadGetStatus(sys_thread_t *);
```

The `sysThreadSelf` service returns the ID of the currently executing thread. Thread priorities may be obtained and adjusted using `sysThreadGetPriority` and `sysThreadSetPriority`. Thread priorities are integer values. The standard Java software thread priority range is defined in the `Thread` class. Special system threads (designated during creation) may use priorities outside the range defined for standard Java software threads.

A thread's set of CPU registers can be obtained by calling `sysThreadRegs`. The complete set of known threads is obtained in an iterative fashion using the `sysThreadEnumerateOver` service. Calling `sysThreadDumpInfo` causes the thread manager to output low-level thread information in a fashion suitable for software development tools to use.

The `sysThreadSizeof` service returns the platform-dependent size of the thread context data structure, and `sysThreadCPUTime` returns statistics regarding the amount of CPU time a thread has used.

Finally, a thread's current execution status is obtained using the `sysThread-GetStatus` service. A thread is always in one of three states: eligible for execution, waiting on a monitor, or waiting on a condition variable associated with a monitor.

9.4.5   Stack Management

The following service returns any thread's current stack pointer:

```
void * sysThreadStackPointer(sys_thread_t *);
```

This service indicates whether a stack overflow condition has occurred for the currently executing thread:

```
int sysThreadCheckStack(void);
```

9.4.6   Software Interrupt and Exception Management

The following services manage threads during interrupt processing.

This service checks to see if a software interrupt is pending for the currently executing thread:

```
int sysInterruptPending(void);
```

This service posts a software interrupt to the designated thread:

```
int sysThreadInterrupt(sys_thread_t *);
```

This service automatically reads, sets, and clears the pending software interrupt flag according to the integer value passed as the second parameter:

```
int sysThreadIsInterrupted(sys_thread_t *, int);
```

This service requests that the thread manager signal an exception for the designated thread:

```
void sysThreadPostException(sys_thread_t *, void *);
```

9.4.7   Thread Manager Clients

The JVM is the primary client of the threading services. Each Java software thread created by the JVM results in an invocation of the `sysThreadCreate` service.

The interrupt manager is the other client of the threading services. Second-level interrupts run in the context of a native thread. Threads that run second-level interrupt handlers are created when the handler is installed and then suspended until the interrupt manager signals a second-level interrupt condition.

9.5   Virtual Memory Manager Services

The VMM provides both page and byte-sized memory management. The VMM (and all JavaOS components) operates under the assumption of a single virtual address space.

9.5.1   Page Management

The page management services used by the JVM are defined as follows:

```
void * sysMapMem(size_t, size_t *);
void * sysUnMapMem(void *, size_t, size_t *);
void * sysCommitMem(void *, size_t, size_t *);
void * sysUnCommitMem(void *, size_t, size_t *);
```

The `size_t` data type is the size of an address on the platform (32 or 64 bits).

Mapping and Unmapping Virtual Memory

The `sysMapMem` service maps a range of virtual memory of the desired size. The pages necessary to back this range of virtual memory are not committed at this time. The amount of mapped memory (a multiple of the page size) is returned.

The `sysUnMapMem` service is used to unmap a range of virtual memory. The range is designated with the starting address and length in bytes. The amount of unmapped memory (a multiple of the page size) is returned.

Committing and Uncommitting Physical Backing Pages

The `sysCommitMem` service requests that physical backing pages be assigned to a range of already mapped virtual memory. The VMM relies on the platform adaptor to supply the necessary physical pages. Physical pages are released by calling the `sysUnCommitMem` service.

I/O Related VMM Services

The JPI memory classes use the microkernel's memory management services to lock and unlock pages in memory, translate addresses, and manipulate the CPU's cache in a platform-independent manner. The page-management services used by the native methods of the JPI are defined as follows.

The `physmap` service maps an area of physical memory, returning a range of virtual memory accessible to device drivers.

```
int physmap(long[] ret, int vasid, long[] paddrs, long[] sizes, long
minaddr, long maxaddr, short alignMask, int cacheMode, boolean
locked, boolean waitformem);
```

The `map` service maps an area of virtual memory, returning a range of virtual memory accessible to device drivers.

```
int map(long[] ret, int vasid, long size, long minaddr, long maxaddr,
short alignMask, int cacheMode, boolean locked, boolean waitformem);
```

The `unmap` service destroys a mapping of virtual memory, previously created by either the `physmap` or `map` service.

```
int unmap(int vasid, long base, long len, int howcreated);
```

The `lock` service makes the pages associated with a mapped region of virtual memory resident in physical memory.

```
int lock(long[] ret, int vasid, long base, long len);
```

The `lockcontig` service makes the pages associated with a mapped region of virtual memory contiguously resident in physical memory.

```
int lockcontig(long[] ret, int vasid, long base, long len);
```

The `unlock` service allows resident pages associated with a mapped region of virtual memory to be released from physical memory.

```
int unlock(int vasid, long base, long len);
```

The `getphys` service returns a scatter-gather list of physical pages associated with a locked region of virtual memory.

```
int getphys(int[] ret, int vasid, long[] pBase, long[] pLen, long
base, long len);
```

The `getcachemode` and `setcachemode` services return and change the current CPU caching mode associated with a range of virtual memory. The modes are defined in the JPI memory classes, as follows (see Chapter 7 for details):

```
void setcachemode(int vasid, long base, long len, int mode);
int getcachemode(int vasid, long base, long len);
```

The `flushcache` service pushes data, code, or both from the CPU's caches into virtual memory.

```
void flushcache(int vasid, long base, long len);
```

These memory services completely align with the needs of the JPI memory classes. For more details on JavaOS memory management, see Chapter 7.

9.5.2 Fine-Grained Memory Management

The following are byte-sized memory management services:

```
void * sysMalloc(size_t);
void * sysRealloc(void *, size_t);
void sysFree(void *);
void * sysCalloc(size_t, size_t);
void * sysAllocBlock(size_t, void **);
```

These functions allocate and free memory in byte-sized chunks, optionally with alignment restrictions. The primary client of these services is the JVM's object manager. The JVM uses both the page-level and byte-level memory management services to manage the size of the object heap (in pages) and the individual objects within the heap (in byte-sized chunks).

JVM build-time options control whether the object heap is preallocated or built dynamically.

9.6 Monitor Manager Services

Most general-purpose microkernels provide more than one kind of synchronization technique to clients. Semaphores, event flags, and Inter-Process Communications (IPC) are among the most common techniques implemented in a microkernel today.

The JVM uses a synchronization technique known as monitors to protect critical regions of Java software and to schedule access to shared data. The JavaOS microkernel provides a highly tuned implementation of monitors to ensure optimum Java software performance.

A monitor is implemented by using a complex data structure with multiple thread queues containing:

- Threads waiting to enter the monitor
- Threads suspended within the monitor
- Threads waiting within the monitor

A monitor has only one owner at a time. Ownership is tracked with a single reference to a thread (a reference to sys_thread_t *). The owning thread can recursively enter the monitor, and each occurrence is tracked by incrementing a count.

Each thread waiting to enter a monitor is waiting to become the next owner of the monitor. Each thread that becomes an owner and is either suspended or waited is also tracked on a queue. Figure 9.4 illustrates the monitor implementation. Each monitor is implemented using a data structure defined as follows:

```
typedef struct sys_mon sys_mon_t;
```

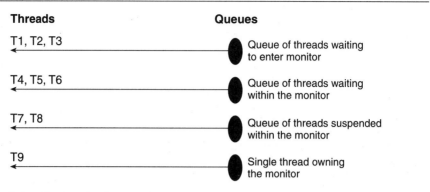

FIGURE 9.4   *Monitor Implementation*

The JVM refers to a monitor by passing references of this type to the microkernel. The complete size and contents of this data structure are platform-dependent and often must take into account CPU details such as cache line size to ensure optimum acquisition and release performance.

9.6.1   Managing Monitors

The JVM instructs the microkernel to create, delete, and return information about monitors using the following microkernel services:

```
size_t sysMonitorSizeof(void);
int sysMonitorInit(sys_mon_t *);
int sysMonitorDestroy(sys_mon_t *);
void sysMonitorDumpInfo(sys_mon_t *);
```

The `sysMonitorSizeof` service returns the size, in bytes, of the microkernel's monitor data structure. The `sysMonitorInit` service creates a monitor and initializes it for use.

To ensure good performance of this important service, the microkernel maintains a cache of ready-to-use monitors. Monitors in the cache are specially marked to prevent deletion of its memory and any associated microkernel resources.

The `sysMonitorDestroy` service deletes a monitor and releases any microkernel resources held by the monitor. The `sysMonitorDumpInfo` service displays the current state of a monitor by printing information to the standard output stream.

9.6.2   Entering a Monitor

Once a monitor is created and initialized, a thread can attempt to become its owner by entering the monitor. Entering the monitor is attempted when the JVM calls the following service in the thread context of the bidding thread:

```
int sysMonitorEnter(sys_thread_t *, sys_mon_t *);
```

If the thread becomes the owner, the following service will return true to the JVM:

```
bool_t sysMonitorEntered(sys_thread_t *, sys_mon_t *);
```

If the monitor already has an owner, the bidding thread is placed on the queue of threads waiting to enter the monitor. This queue (and all the other thread queues) is ordered from highest- to lowest-priority thread.

9.6.3   Exiting a Monitor

Ownership of a monitor is revoked by exiting the monitor. A thread exits a monitor when the virtual machine invokes the following microkernel service:

```
int sysMonitorExit(sys_thread_t *, sys_mon_t *);
```

Exiting a monitor causes the microkernel to check the queue for bidding threads. If that queue is not empty, the thread at the head of the queue becomes the new monitor owner. Otherwise, the microkernel returns the monitor to the monitor cache.

9.6.4   Waiting Within a Monitor

Sometimes threads wait (or block) within a monitor until a notification condition is signaled. Threads can optionally specify a maximum wait time (a 64-bit number of milliseconds).

A thread waits within a monitor when the virtual machine invokes the following microkernel service:

```
int sysMonitorWait(sys_thread_t *, sys_mon_t *, int64_t);
```

Waiting a monitor causes the microkernel to verify that the current thread is indeed the current owner of the monitor. An error condition is returned if this is not the case.

Next, the microkernel checks to see if a maximum timeout value was specified. If so, a timer is set on behalf of the current thread.

Finally, the current thread is placed on the queue of waiting threads.

9.6.5   Notifying Waiting Threads

The JVM uses two different services to wake up threads waiting within a monitor. The first service wakes only the highest-priority thread (the one at the head of the wait queue). The other service wakes up all waiting threads.

```
int sysMonitorNotify(sys_thread_t *, sys_mon_t *);
int sysMonitorNotifyAll(sys_thread_t *, sys_mon_t *);
```

Before waking up any threads, the microkernel checks that the thread designated by the first parameter is indeed the owner of the monitor.

9.7   File Manager Services

The JVM requires a file system to hold class files. The JavaOS microkernel supports a simple native file system that is used to bootstrap the OS until more sophisticated Java software file systems in the runtime layer become active.

The bootstrap file system's contents are defined using two methods. The first method defines file system contents during the JavaOS build process. A tool called a Filizer processes a list of files. The output of the Filizer is a data structure containing the file contents and a directory header that indexes the contents. The JavaOS file manager exports a POSIX-like file interface layered on top of this directory header.

The second method is to designate files to be loaded by the booter (see Chapter 10) and subsequently dynamically inserted into the bootstrap file system during the booting process.

During start-up, the file manager requests a list of files (using the JBI) to be inserted into the bootstrap file system.

The file manager's file interface used by the JVM consists of the following services:

`int sysIsAbsolute(const char *path);` returns true if the pathname is absolute as opposed to a relative pathname.

`int sysAccess(const char *path, int permission);` returns true if the file is accessible using the specified permission value (read, write).

`int sysStat(const char *path, struct stat *status);` returns file status.

`int sysOpen(const char *fileName, int openMode, int permission);` opens the specified file in a given mode.

`int sysClose(int fd);` closes an open file.

`long sysSeek(int fd, long offset, int whence);` moves the read/write pointer within the file's contents.

`int sysSetLength(int fd, int64_t length);` sets a file to a specified length.

`int sysSync(int fd);` synchronizes a file's cached contents with a file's persistent contents.

`int sysAvailable(int fd, long *bytes);` returns true if the file is available to read and, if so, sets the file's size to the number of bytes specified in the second parameter.

`size_t sysRead(int fd, void *buf, unsigned int nBytes);` reads bytes from a file.

`size_t sysWrite(int fd, const void *buf, unsigned int nBytes);` writes bytes to a file.

`int sysRename(const char *srcName, const char *dstName);` changes the name of a file.

`int sysUnlink(const char *file);` deletes a file.

`int sysMkdir(const char *path, int mode);` creates a directory.

`int sysRmdir(const char *path, char *result, int result_len);` deletes a directory.

`int sysCanonicalPath(char *path, char *result, int result_len);` returns the canonical form of the pathname.

9.8 Library Manager Services

The library manager loads native code libraries in response to requests from the JVM. The JVM requires the following services to dynamically load and link native code libraries:

`void sysBuildLibName(char *, int, char *, char *);` creates a C string suitable for naming a library to load by adding the appropriate pathname prefix and filename extensions.

`int sysBuildFunName(char *, int, int, int);` builds a library function name that can be used to find a function symbol within a library.

`long *sysInvokeNative(void *, void *, long *, char *, int, void *);` calls a native function within a library.

`void *sysLoadLibrary(const char *);` loads a native code library into memory.

`void sysUnloadLibrary(void *);` unloads a native code library.

`void *sysFindLibraryEntry(void *, const char *);` finds a symbol within a library.

`void *sysFindBuiltinEntry(const char *);` finds a symbol in the native code not found in a loadable library.

9.9   JVM Management Services

The following services are used to start, initialize, and stop the JVM:

int sysSetOption(void *); sets a platform-specific JVM startup option.

int sysGetDefaultPaths(char **java_home, char **class_path, char **lib_path); returns the default directory pathnames to the home directory, the set of class directories, and the native code library directory.

int sysInitializeJavaVM(); executes JVM's platform-specific initialization sequence.

int sysFinalizeJavaVM(void *); executes JVM's platform-specific shutdown sequence.

sys_props *sysGetProperties(); returns a pointer to a sys_props data structure containing the set of standard Java system property values.

9.10   Startup and Shutdown Manager Services

The JavaOS startup and shutdown procedures are activated using the following services:

```
int start_JavaOS(int bootOpsID, void *JBIfunctions);
void stop_JavaOS(char *reason);
```

The JBI-compliant booter invokes the startup procedure. (See Chapter 10 for details.) The stop procedure is invoked after the JVM terminates or if an unhandled OS error is encountered.

9.11   Summary

The JavaOS microkernel is a small native component of the OS that is hidden well beneath the JPI. The microkernel's role is to provide highly tuned services to the JVM and to the JPI native methods.

The JavaOS microkernel is simpler than many microkernels, yielding a more portable and efficient implementation of the Java application execution environment.

Chapter 10
Booting

Booting is the process of placing the operating system in control of the hardware. Booting is among the more arcane software processes, occurring at the lowest levels of the system for a short period of time. Application software never interacts with the booter, so you might wonder why we include a chapter on booting at all. The reason is to show how JavaOS has been designed to boot from many different platforms, from network computers to PCs to embedded devices.

10.1   The JavaOS Boot Interface

JavaOS works with a variety of booters. To boot JavaOS, a booter must perform four basic steps:

1. Load the initial JavaOS application environment into executable memory
2. Cede control to the JavaOS Runtime Enviroment
3. Identify the platform configuration to JavaOS
4. Uninstall itself from memory when its job is complete

Regardless of the underlying booting implementation, a standard interface layer called the JavaOS Boot Interface (JBI) carries out these four basic steps. The JBI consists of C function calls for ceding control to JavaOS, exchanging platform configuration information, and uninstalling the booter. Examples of booters that the JBI supports are:

- Network booters, which load and run JavaOS from a network
- Hard disk booters, which load and run JavaOS from a hard disk

- Floppy disk booters, which load and run JavaOS from a floppy disk
- Flash RAM/ROM booters, which load and run JavaOS from flash memory

Broadly, the JBI is divided into two categories of functions: those that transfer control to JavaOS once the booter has installed enough of the OS image to make transfer possible, and those that allow JavaOS to request platform configuration information from the booter once JavaOS is running.

10.2   Starting JavaOS

Once the booter has installed enough of the OS image to transfer control, the booter calls a known entry point in the JavaOS boot image to start JavaOS. This is called the *startup entry point*. The startup entry point receives a number of parameters from the booter. These parameters define the initial JavaOS execution environment and let JavaOS know where and how to request configuration information from the booter.

The first parameter is a value called the *bootops ID*, which JavaOS passes to the booter on subsequent function calls. Think of this ID as a ticket to platform configuration information from the booter. Its actual value is not important; JavaOS simply stores the value for return to the booter on subsequent function calls.

Function calls to the booter are accomplished through a table of entry points. One of the parameters to the startup entry point is a pointer to this table of booter entry points. Each entry point has its own unique parameters, but one parameter common to all entry points is the bootops ID. The calling syntax of the entry points follows the C calling syntax.

Once JavaOS gets control from the booter, the OS begins to execute. JavaOS requires an initial stack environment of suitable size for holding parameters and return values for function calls. Before transferring control, the booter places JavaOS on an *initial stack* and passes the startup entry point a pointer to the first byte of the stack. The booter also passes the size, in bytes, of the initial stack. JavaOS uses this stack initially, but eventually sets up its own. The booter cannot assume that the initial stack is the one that JavaOS will be using when it later invokes the booter functions. The OS might have switched to its own stack by then. The booter functions minimize the use of stack space because when they execute, they cannot know the available stack space.

The last usable byte of the initial stack is at the address:

```
stack start address + stack size - 1
```

The initial stack must be aligned on a 32-byte boundary and ideally should be a multiple of the CPU page size. A minimum initial stack size of 16KB is required to provide an ample environment for JavaOS execution, as well as to allow stack space for calls to the booter functions (if JavaOS has not switched to its own stack first).

Figure 10.1 indicates the relationship between the stack address, stack size, and top of stack. In configuration (A) the stack pointer is decremented to push new elements onto the stack, and in configuration (B) the stack pointer is incremented for push operations.

For configuration (A), top = $stackAddr + stackLength - 1$. For configuration (B), top = $stackAddr$. Whether the system uses configuration (A) or (B) depends on the nature of the CPU and addressing scheme. JavaOS supports both configurations.

Once JavaOS establishes its own stack environment, it reclaims the initial stack memory for other purposes. Once the startup entry point is called, the booter must assume that the initial stack memory belongs to JavaOS and, thus, must never try to allocate from the stack or use the stack to store variables, except to pass parameters to JavaOS when the startup routine is invoked.

Once the OS startup entry point is invoked, the booter's use of memory is limited to the ranges that the booter assigned to itself before the entry point was invoked. Within these assigned ranges the booter can safely allocate and free memory, but it cannot take over new ranges to which it was not previously assigned because JavaOS might have begun using these other regions for its own purposes.

JavaOS should never return from the call to the startup entry routine. Once ready, JavaOS asks the booter to uninstall itself from memory and then takes over the system entirely. JavaOS returning to the booter from the entry point call signifies the occurrence of a serious and unrecoverable error condition.

Figures 10.2, 10.3, and 10.4 illustrate the high-level view of the JavaOS booting sequences. The booter must disable all device interrupts prior to invoking the

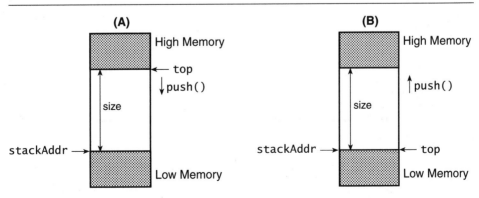

FIGURE 10.1 *Stack Relationship*

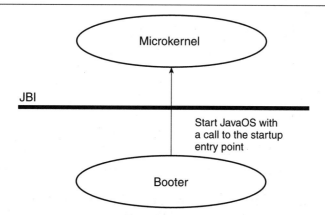

FIGURE 10.2 *JavaOS Booting Sequence A*

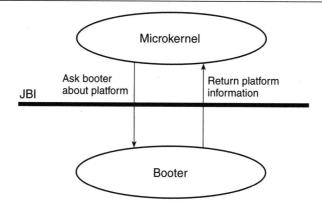

FIGURE 10.3 *JavaOS Booting Sequence B*

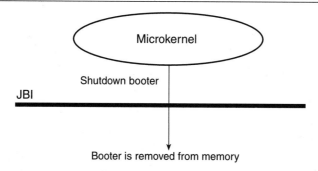

FIGURE 10.4 *JavaOS Booting Sequence C*

startup entry point. Additionally, the booter must suspend all I/O, such as DMA and programmed I/O, before JavaOS is entered. Once the booter is removed from memory, JavaOS reclaims all of the memory the booter either occupied or controlled.

Typically, the hardware manufacturer installs the booter on the system. On the other hand, downstream distributors or the end user can install and reinstall JavaOS. For this reason, it is crucial that the booter and JavaOS have a means of determining version compatibilities. A later version of JavaOS may require functions that an early-version booter does not implement. To solve this problem, the booter returns a version number to JavaOS used to determine which functions are available. If the version number indicates an incompatible booter, booting fails and an earlier version of JavaOS must be installed on the system. Earlier versions will work with later booter versions because later versions always must implement a superset of the functions in earlier versions.

10.3   Retrieving Platform Configuration Information

Once JavaOS is in control, it calls the booter to obtain information about the platform it is running on. Platform configuration information includes:

- A physical system memory map
- A virtual system memory map
- Platform device information

Platform devices include one or more CPUs, buses, network adaptors, and video adaptors. The booter returns information about platform devices in the form of *device entries,* which are not to be confused with entries in the JSD `Device` namespace described in Chapter 4. They are distinct entities although both types of entry contain similar information, such as name, value, and optional properties list. Among other differences, a booter device entry is a C structure, but a `Device` namespace entry is a Java object.

10.3.1   Calling Booter Functions

Rather than invoking a booter function directly, JavaOS makes a call to a C wrapper function, which in turn invokes the entry point for the function. The booter must implement all the entry points in the table. If the booter does not support a particular function, it must provide an empty implementation (a stub function) and a valid entry point. JavaOS does not check the entries in the table for nullity.

Figure 10.5 illustrates a call to a booter function, first through the wrapper, then to the table, and finally to the entry point itself. Once the booter is removed from memory, its functions do not simply vanish. For reasons of timing and simplicity, JavaOS replicates its functions internally. This way, if other system services need what the booter provides, they obtain the information directly from JavaOS, without concern as to whether the calls are made before or after the booter is removed from memory.

JavaOS builds its own set of data structures as it calls the booter functions. As a result, once the booter is removed, JavaOS can mimic its functions through the C wrapper functions. This is why the wrapper functions are so useful—the booter functions are called through the wrappers, and the caller never needs to know whether the booter is actually resident.

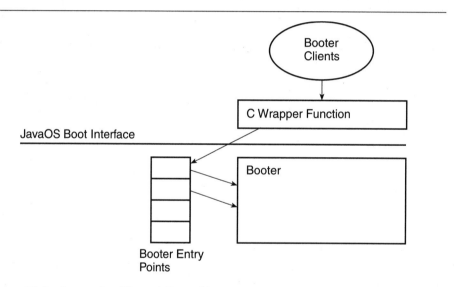

FIGURE 10.5 *Invocation Flow of Control in* `BootOps`

10.3.2 Physical Memory Map

The configuration information returned by the booter includes the layout of physical memory in the system. A *range* of physical memory is defined by a starting physical address and size, a type, and an owner. A physical memory range can have one of the following types:

- *Read-only.* ROM memory.
- *Random access.* RAM memory.

- *Non-valid.* No memory exists in this range.
- *Fixed I/O.* Memory range is assigned to fixed I/O devices.
- *Expansion I/O.* Memory range is assigned to expansion I/O devices.
- *Reserved.* Reserved for system use.

Non-valid memory ranges do not have physical memory backing them (memory holes). *Fixed I/O* ranges are used by fixed I/O devices, video cards, or serial port controllers, for instance. *Expansion I/O* ranges are reserved for installable expansion devices such as peripheral adaptors.

A pointer describes each range of physical memory to the starting address and the length of the range in bytes. Each range also is assigned an owner. The owner is the software component that occupies or controls the memory. Possible owners are JavaOS, the booter, or neither one (free memory). Only the owner can use or deallocate the memory in the range.

The booter returns attributes of a physical memory range—starting address and size, type, and owner—in the form of a data structure. The entire physical memory map of the system is returned as an array of these data structures. Figure 10.6 illustrates a sample physical memory map that the booter returns.

The array of physical memory map entries is allocated from booter memory. The entries in the array are ordered by their starting address. Each of the ten array entries in the figure denotes the range type, current owner of the range (JavaOS, booter, free), starting address, and range length.

In the figure, both the booter and JavaOS own ranges in physical memory. There is a small memory hole at 0x9f000. Only 64MB of RAM is installed, so a large memory hole starts at 0x4000000. Additionally, a PROM is installed in the upper 2MB of the physical address space, and just below it lies 14MB of memory-mapped I/O addresses.

10.3.3 Virtual Memory Map

The booter also is responsible for telling JavaOS the layout of virtual memory in the system. If the system has a memory-management unit, the layout of virtual memory might be quite different from the layout of physical memory. For this reason, the booter must provide a virtual memory map to supplement the physical memory map.

Like physical memory ranges, virtual memory ranges have a starting physical address and a length. Each virtual range also is assigned a starting virtual address corresponding to the starting physical address. A caching mode is assigned to each range to indicate how the CPU can cache the pages in that range. Valid caching modes are write-back, write-through, and noncachable.

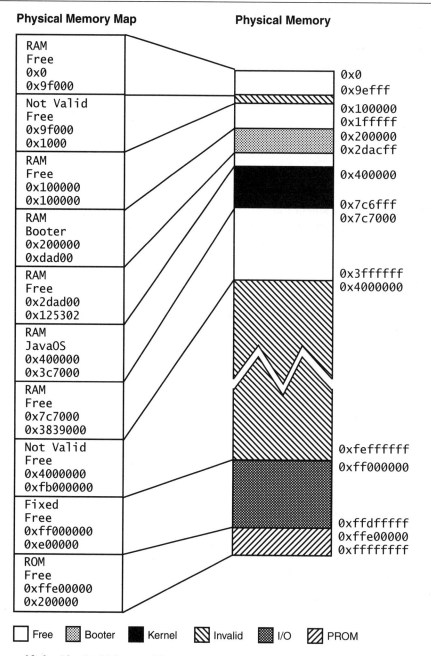

FIGURE 10.6   *Physical Memory Map*

The virtual memory map returned by the booter is an array of entries, each representing a range of virtual memory. The entries in the array are organized in ascending order by starting virtual address. Within a given range of virtual memory, the addresses must be both physically and virtually contiguous. However, there is no requirement that two virtual ranges adjacent in the map be physically contiguous in the system. Nor is there a requirement that every physical range in the system be mapped to a virtual range. When the starting physical and virtual addresses for a range are the same, the range is said to be *identity-mapped*.

Consider the physical memory map in Figure 10.6. Assume that the booter has identity-mapped itself, the I/O address range, and the PROM, and that the microkernel has been mapped according to the virtual addresses specified in its executable file header. If the microkernel text is mapped in at 0xf8000000 and its DATA and BSS segments are mapped to 0xf8600000, then, assuming CPU support for write-back caching, Figure 10.7 shows the corresponding virtual memory map.

```
WriteBack
0x200000
0x200000
0xdad00
```
```
WriteBack
0xf8000000
0x400000
0x384000
```
```
WriteBack
0xf8600000
0x784000
0x4300
```
```
NonCachable
0xff000000
0xff000000
0xe00000
```
```
NonCachable
0xffe00000
0xffe00000
0x200000
```

FIGURE 10.7 *Virtual Memory Map*

10.3.4 File Augmentation

The booter may augment JavaOS with one or more files downloaded at boot time. This feature is optional. When implemented, the booter loads the files into memory along with JavaOS before passing control to the startup entry point. When network booting is used, the booter and the network server the system boots from work together to identify and download the additional files.

The file augmentation feature is useful for downloading Java software classes, packages, and system services, such as device drivers, at boot time. These downloaded files are automatically appended to the JavaOS ROM (bootstrap) file system and become part of the JavaOS Runtime Environment for that particular system.

10.3.5   Platform Device Configuration

The platform device configuration is conveyed from the booter to JavaOS using a data structure called the *device tree*. (Although the two contain very similar information, the device tree should not be confused with the Device namespace in the JSD.) The device tree is a C structure constructed by the booter at boot time or earlier, possibly hardcoded into ROM or stored on the server. The entries in the device tree are limited to devices that the booter knows about or can discover. The JSD Device namespace, on the other hand, is a linked collection of Java objects representing not only fixed and expansion platform devices, but also devices that might have been added after booting, such as PC/MCIA cards.

Figure 10.8 illustrates the booter's device tree. The top-level entry is the *root* of the tree, representing one or more system CPUs. The direct children of the root represent system-level buses, such as PCI, SBus, and ISA. The third level consists of physical devices (SVGA, network adaptor, SCSI host adaptor, and so on).

Like entries in the JSD, device tree entries have a name and value, and contain references to their parent, siblings, and left-most child. Optionally, they can have one or more properties.

The property name is an ASCII string. A name consists of from 1 to 31 printable characters, as defined by the IEEE 1275–1994 standard. Names cannot contain uppercase characters or include the characters /, \, :, [,], or @. Property names

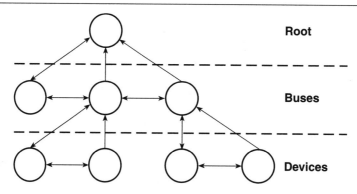

FIGURE 10.8 *Booter Device Tree*

beginning with the character + are reserved for use by future revisions of the IEEE 1275 standard.

Properties are important because they provide JavaOS with details about the device. Each property is a name-value pair, where the value is generally an array of zero or more bytes. A zero-length property value is used when the property represents a Boolean state with a presence (true) or absence (false). Values are represented in big-endian format. Even the name of the device entry is simply a property with a name-value pair of `name-<device name>`, such as `name-CPU`.

10.4   Device Discovery

JavaOS is not particular about how the device tree comes into existence: Its creation is entirely up to the booter. Some elaborate boot PROMs, such as OpenBoot, scan the system for devices and build the tree dynamically. When layered upon OpenBoot, JavaOS relies on the OpenBoot PROM to do all the work of device discovery. Other booters, especially those for embedded applications, might take a simpler approach and hardcode the tree into a C structure, maintain it in flash memory, or retrieve it from the server. The bus managers maintaining the `Device` namespace can perform their own device discovery to supplement deficiencies in a booter-supplied device tree.

JavaOS uses the booter's functions to copy the device tree from the booter memory into the Java Runtime Environment heap as entries in the JSD `Device` namespace (you knew they were related!). During this copy operation, JavaOS might edit or append information in the device entry. Once the tree is copied into the `Device` namespace, JavaOS can remove the booter from memory and begin matching bus managers and device drivers with devices in the tree.

10.5   Preboot Execution Environment Standard

JavaOS accommodates many kinds of booting subsystems, including a new one defined by Intel. The Intel Preboot Execution Environment (PXE)[1] booting standard defines a booting process for networked thin-clients (NCs). Specifically, PXE defines the NC operating environment until an executable file containing an operating system (or OS booter program) can be downloaded from the server. JavaOS supports a PXE-compliant booting system.

---

1. PXE is compliant with PCI local bus specifications and is a NET PC standard. For more information on the PXE booting standard, see the following Web site: `http://developer.intel.com/ial/WfM/design/pxedt/dhcp.htm`.

Following the PXE booting standard, information passes between the client NC and the server, through the standard Dynamic Host Configuration Protocol (DHCP). This information includes an IP address assigned to the client NC by the server, and an executable boot file sent to the client NC by means of the Trivial File Transfer Protocol (TFTP) standard.

The executable boot file (booter) is placed in memory on the client NC. Once the booter executes, it defines the remaining booting process. PXE-compliant booting requires support from networking cards. PXE-compliant ROMs residing on an Ethernet or Token Ring card adhere to a well-defined interface understood by the booter and the machine's BIOS.

10.6   Summary

The JBI provides a standard interface to diverse booting systems. Booters must implement all functions defined in the JBI but have some flexibility in omitting functionality, such as file augmentation.

The booting system is a native code component that implements the JBI. The booting system can be tailored to suit virtually any environment, including the use of flash RAM/ROM for booting and custom PROMs for embedded devices, such as modems or phones. Some JavaOS booter implementations may leverage an existing PROM standard, such as OpenBoot, PXE, or PC-BIOS.

Index

Addison-Wesley Computer and Engineering Publishing Group

How to Interact with Us

1. Visit our Web site

http://www.awl.com/cseng

When you think you've read enough, there's always more content for you at Addison-Wesley's web site. Our web site contains a directory of complete product information including:

- Chapters
- Exclusive author interviews
- Links to authors' pages
- Tables of contents
- Source code

You can also discover what tradeshows and conferences Addison-Wesley will be attending, read what others are saying about our titles, and find out where and when you can meet our authors and have them sign your book.

2. Subscribe to Our Email Mailing Lists

Subscribe to our electronic mailing lists and be the first to know when new books are publishing. Here's how it works: Sign up for our electronic mailing at **http://www.awl.com/cseng/mailinglists.html**. Just select the subject areas that interest you and you will receive notification via email when we publish a book in that area.

3. Contact Us via Email

cepubprof@awl.com
Ask general questions about our books.
Sign up for our electronic mailing lists.
Submit corrections for our web site.

bexpress@awl.com
Request an Addison-Wesley catalog.
Get answers to questions regarding your order or our products.

innovations@awl.com
Request a current Innovations Newsletter.

webmaster@awl.com
Send comments about our web site.

mikeh@awl.com
Submit a book proposal.
Send errata for an Addison-Wesley book.

cepubpublicity@awl.com
Request a review copy for a member of the media interested in reviewing new Addison-Wesley titles.

We encourage you to patronize the many fine retailers who stock Addison-Wesley titles. Visit our online directory to find stores near you or visit our online store: **http://store.awl.com/** or call **800-824-7799**.

Addison Wesley Longman
Computer and Engineering Publishing Group
One Jacob Way, Reading, Massachusetts 01867 USA
TEL 781-944-3700 • FAX 781-942-3076